Revealing The Revelation Of Jesus Christ

Blessed *is* he that readeth, and
they that hear the words of
this prophecy, and keep
those things which are
written therein: for
the time is
at hand.
Revelation 1:3

Bill Hathaway DD

Copyright © 2024 Bill Hathaway DD
All cover art copyright © 2024 Bill Hathaway DD
All Rights Reserved

No part of this book may be reproduced or transmitted in any form or by any means, electronic or mechanical, including photocopying, recording, or by any information storage and retrieval system, without permission in writing from the author.

REVEALING
THE REVELATION
OF JESUS CHRIST
(A SEVEN-SUNDAY SERIES)

Publishing Coordinator – Sharon Kizziah-Holmes

Paperback-Press
an imprint of A & S Publishing
Paperback Press, LLC
Springfield, Missouri

ISBN -13: 978-1-960499-76-9

DEDICATION

I would like to dedicate this book on the Revelation to Pastor Gary E. Longstaff. It was his suggestion to name this book, "Revealing the Revelation." Bro. Gary has been an inspiration and encouragement to me for many years. I am proud to call him "My Pastor." this book is the result of Pastor Gary asking me to preach a seven-week series on the Revelation. At that time, I had no idea of writing a book.

CONTENTS

Dedication	iii
Acknowledgments	i
Foreword	i
Preface	iii
Facts About the Book of Revelation	iv
Introduction	vii
Chapter 1	1
Chapter 2	5
1. The first church – Ephesus	5
2. The second church – Smyrna	6
3. The third church – Pergamos	7
4. The Fourth Church -Thyatira	7
Chapter 3	9
5. The Fifth Church – Sardis	9
6. The Sixth Church	10
7. The Seventh Church – Laodicean Church	11
Chapter 4	13
Chapter 5	17
Chapter 6	21
First Seal	24
Second Seal	25
Third Seal	25
Fourth Seal	26
Fifth Seal	28
Sixth Seal	29
Chapter 7	33
Chapter 8	37
Seventh Seal	37
The First Trumpet	38
The Second Trumpet	38
The Third Trumpet	39
The Fourth Trumpet	39
Chapter 9	41
The Fifth Trumpet	41

  The Sixth Trumpet 42
Chapter 10 45
Chapter 11 49
Chapter 12 55
Chapter 13 61
Chapter 14 71
Chapter 15 77
Chapter 16 79
  The First Bowl 80
  The Second Bowl 81
  The Third Bowl 82
  The Fourth Bowl 82
  The Fifth Bowl 83
  The Sixth Bowl 84
  The Seventh Bowl 89
Chapter 17 91
Chapter 18 97
Chapter 19 103
Chapter 20 111
Chapter 21 117
Chapter 22 121
About the Author 128

ACKNOWLEDGMENTS

I believe "Encouragement Is the Transfer Of Strength." At 93, I realize I cannot do some of the things I used to do, but I've asked the Lord to help me continue serving Him until He calls me home. I thank many who pray for me. I thank my four kids, Ike, Paul, Jim and Ruth for their love and encouragement. I also thank my wife Margaret's son Robert, and daughter Rita, for all the help they've given me since Margaret relocated to heaven. I thank the Lord for helping me overcome much physical pain. I believe "I can do all things through Christ, which strengtheneth me." Thank you all for your love and prayers. God bless you as you read this book.

FOREWORD
By Pastor Gary Longstaff

I have known the author of this book, Dr. Bill Hathaway for over 50 years. Most recently our relationship is as his pastor. He is a blessing to our church and to all who also call him friend. This book is a result of my asking if he could take us through The Revelation in seven sermons. He accepted the challenge successfully.

This compilation will give the reader a complete look at this book of The Bible that is of great importance, especially in this day. Bro. Bill was able to capture the text, teachings, and theme without losing the reader in deep detail that can dissuade some would be students and those seeking a "refresher course." However, he still maintained sound doctrine and teaching of the deep themes that have intrigued Christians and prophecy students for centuries.

My prayer is this book will be a blessing to you as the reader and perhaps any who come to it seeking truth and insight into the days in which we live and the days that are without doubt coming?

Pastor Gary Longstaff
Grandview Baptist Church
Springfield, Missouri

PREFACE

Dear Reader:

About a week or two after I surrendered as a missionary in 1951, while stationed in Japan, Missionary Ike Foster took me to Tokyo. He said I needed to get experience preaching.

I preached my first message in 1951 on a street corner in Tokyo using an interpreter. I wore my army uniform. Recently, when I was asked by Pastor Gary Longstaff if I would consider teaching a 7-Sunday series on the Revelation, after much prayer, I accepted the challenge.

Over the years, I have studied and preached much on the Revelation. It has always thrilled me and captured my attention. I have prayed for the Holy Spirit to reveal the true meaning of the book. For sure, I am not known as a prophecy speaker. I have to read a lot, study much, pray much and depend on the Holy Spirit to guide me. In preparation for writing this 7-Sunday series, I have gone over many years of material.

There are a few places in this book, such as the synopsis of the beast and his activities starting on page 66 that I gleaned from others. I include this information because it makes things clear, and I would not be able to write it better. I thank the Lord that at 93, God has enabled me to continue preaching and serving my Lord and Savior Jesus Christ. May you receive a blessing as you read this book. I am using the KJV Bible for all scriptures.

Bill Hathaway, Missionary to Japan

FACTS ABOUT THE BOOK OF REVELATION

1. Who wrote the Book? John, inspired by God wrote the Book of the Revelation (Rev. 1:1). *"The Revelation of Jesus Christ, which God gave unto him, to shew unto his servants things which must shortly come to pass: and he signified it by his angel unto his servant John."* Therefore, the Book of the Revelation is God-inspired and written by John.

2. To whom was the Book written? Rev. 1:4 tells us it was written to the 7 churches in Asia, not the Asia we know of today. Today we know it as Asia Minor.

3. When was the Book written? It was written in the first century when there was horrible persecution of Christians.

4. Where was the Book written? It was written while John was in exile on the isle of Patmos, because of his testimony for Jesus Christ.

5. Why was the Book written? It is evident in the Revelation that the purpose was to encourage Christians throughout the centuries of time.

6. The Book of Revelation has 7 visions.

(1) The vision of Christ.
(2) The vision of the seals.
(3) The vision of the trumpets.
(4) The vision of the personages.
(5) The vision of the 7 vials or bowls.
(6) The vision of the 7 dooms.
(7) The vision of 7 new things.

Now we enter into the very first chapter of The Revelation. I pray this study will thrill your hearts and cause you to become stronger in the Lord.

INTRODUCTION

I am a semi-retired missionary to Japan with a Japanese ministry in the Grandview Baptist Church in Springfield, Missouri. When Pastor Gary Longstaff asked me if I would consider teaching a seven-week series through the Revelation, I knew it would be a challenge. It became an opportunity. As a missionary and pastor, I had taught the entire 22 chapters of the Revelation several times. To narrow down these years of study into just 7 lessons took quite a while to decide. <u>I have found it to be inspiring, informative, exhaustive, alarming, thrilling, instructive, exciting, warning and the most impressive book that I have ever studied.</u> I will tell you that if you do not read and study the Revelation of Jesus Christ, you are missing the greatest blessing. I see why there is a special blessing given to those who read, hear, and keep the words of this book. The word "revelation" is sometimes called "<u>The Apocalypse,</u>" which literally means an unveiling, or manifestation. Jesus Christ is the one great theme. It reveals Him as the Lamb rejected, and soon to reign in glory – The Lamb on the throne! <u>I urge you not to miss one lesson</u>. It so captured my attention that I did not like interruptions. I will do my best to keep your interest. I want to make it come alive. Pray every day that I will make it so interesting that you can't wait for the next lesson.

Bill Hathaway

CHAPTER 1

<u>VERSE 1</u>: "The Revelation" – singular: not plural.
There is but one Revelation revealing the message of the <u>appearing of Christ</u>. We are looking for His appearing at the Rapture (4:1). There is a day coming when every eye shall see Him at the hour of His return to earth (1:7). The word "shortly" means "rapidity of action once there is a beginning." The newspapers today report about things showing His return will be soon. One such important event was when Israel became a nation on May 14,1948, after about 2000 years of obscurity. I quote from the internet:

US President Harry Truman recognized Israel as a nation. Here's the internet's information on this subject: "Nov 6, 2022 — Indeed, more than three and a quarter of a million people have "made Aliyah" since 1948. Jews to leave, many of whom settled in Israel." They came from the north, east, south, and west. Listen to this: Isaiah
43:5-6, *"Fear not: for I am with thee: I will bring thy seed from the east and gather thee from the west; I will say to the north, Give up; and to the south, Keep not back: bring my sons from far, and my daughters from the*

ends of the earth."

VERSE 2: John tells only what he saw.

VERSE 3: Here is a special blessing given to those who read and keep what is written in the Book. If you want the greatest blessings ever, spend time in the Book of The Revelation.

VERSE 4: John now turns his attention to the 7 local churches in Asia; we know them as Asia Minor.

VERSE 5: *"And from Jesus Christ who is the faithful witness, the first begotten of the dead..."* Why is Christ the first begotten from the dead, when Lazarus and others were raised first? Others were raised to life only to die again. That's the difference.

VERSE 6: *"Hath made us kings and priests ..."* 1 Pet. 2:9 *"But ye are a chosen generation, <u>a royal priesthood</u>, an holy nation, a peculiar people; that ye should shew forth the praises of him who hath called you out of darkness into his marvelous light."*

VERSE 7: The theme of Revelation is Jesus Christ and his appearance through eternity. The rapture as indicated in 4:1.

VERSE 8: Jesus is talking. <u>He is the *"Alpha and Omega, the beginning and the end."*</u> Jesus is telling us that He is the omnipotent Almighty God. He is the one and only God, the creator of heaven and earth. and that He is the great

"I AM."

VERSE 9: John is merely stating that he is a "brother, and companion in tribulation," with the other brothers and sisters in Christ. John was banished to the isle of Patmos because of his uncompromising testimony. He was different. He was a separatist! There is nothing wrong with being separate from the world, the flesh and the devil and being separate to God. It takes real determination and commitment to take such a stand.

VERSE 10: John states that he was *in the Spirit on the Lord's Day*. What's that telling us? We too, need to be so faithful and attend church on the Lord's Day and not let anything stop us. Our neighbors need to see our determination to observe His day. Your testimony may help them realize that the Bible is true. Don't you think when John was all alone in silence, that the voice and trumpet he suddenly heard made him jump? It would me. I know it got his full attention. WOW!

VERSE 11: This verse emphasizes verse 8.

VERSES 12-16: The description of what he saw. I will read these verses. I cannot describe it better than as it is written. 1:12 And *I turned to see the voice that spake with me. And being turned, I saw seven golden candlesticks;* (here is a description of Jesus Christ). 13 *And in the midst of the seven candlesticks one like unto the Son of man, clothed with a garment down to the foot* (That's his priestly garment), *and girt about the paps with a golden girdle* (speaks of service). 14 *His head and his hairs were white like wool, as white as snow* (symbol of His holiness); *and his eyes were as a flame of fire* (indicating his omniscience); 15 *And his feet like unto fine brass* (brass was the strongest metal at that time (symbol of judgment), *as if they burned in a furnace; and his voice as the sound of many waters* (symbolizes His authority over the entire world). 16 And he had in his right hand seven stars: *and out of his mouth went a sharp two-edged sword:* (symbol of the Word of God), *and his countenance was as the sun shineth in his strength* (pictures the glory of Christ). Notice Rev. 1:20 *"The mystery of the seven stars which thou sawest in my right hand, and the seven golden candlesticks. <u>The seven stars are the angels of the seven churches: and the seven candlesticks which thou sawest are the seven churches."</u>* The word of God, Hebrews 4:12 states *"For the word of God is quick, and powerful, and sharper than any two-edged sword, piercing even to the dividing asunder of soul and spirit, and of the joints and marrow, and is a discerner of the thoughts and intents of the heart."*

<u>VERSES 17-18</u>: The shock of hearing all this caused John to fall down in great shock almost like he died. Then Jesus speaks to him, *"Fear not; I am the first and the last. I am he that liveth, and was dead; behold, I am alive forever, Amen; and have the keys of hell and of death."* Jesus has the keys of hell and death, meaning our life is in His hands.

<u>VERSE 19</u>: John is given the command to write <u>what he saw,</u> and <u>the things that are,</u> and <u>the things that shall be.</u> Past, present, and future.

Chapter 2

I. THE SEVEN CHURCHES

These seven churches existed during John's time, but they also represent the condition of future churches during certain years of history.

1. The first church – Ephesus

AD 70 - 170. The Backslidden Church (2:1-7). There was much persecution of Christians during that time. During this time Nero, perhaps the most horrible, notorious ruthless tyrant of history lived. He even put his mother to death. Also, he slew Octavia, his wife. He is accused of burning Rome. Nero ordered that Christians should be rounded up and killed. Some were torn apart by lions. Others were burned alive as human torches. Despite such cruel persecution, the churches continued to grow. How he died is not known, but I believe God took his life at age 30. Christians have always gone through much persecution. Church buildings were destroyed, but the Church of Jesus Christ will last forever. The building is not a church. The church consists of its body of believers.

Their condemnation: *"Thou hast left thy first love"* (2:4). They had some good points, but they are remembered for the bad points. Isn't that true today? A person can live a good life for 70, 80 or 90 years, but do one terrible thing and be remembered for the one bad thing.

2. The second church – Smyrna

AD 170-AD 312. The Persecuted Church or The Loyal Church (2:8-11). During this time, the church went through 10 persecutions under 10 horrible rulers. During this period and throughout church history, some churches became known by such names as Novatians, Montanists, Paulicians, as well as Christians (Acts 11:26). <u>This line of churches which started with Jesus and the disciples became known as the present Baptist Church because they insisted on baptizing new believers</u>. These churches were given the name "Ana-Baptist, or Re-Baptizers because they

would not accept new members from the Catholic Church." It was the Catholic Church that called the Baptist Church "Ana-Baptist" in derision; Ana-Baptist means "re-baptizers." The Catholic Church started about AD 300, many years after the Baptist Church. In time the "Ana" was dropped resulting in the name "Baptist" remained. During this time the Smyrna church members were fed to the lions at Rome while many cheered. <u>It is claimed that over 5 million Christians were murdered during this period.</u> But the church continued to grow. It did not cease to exist, and never will.

3. The third church – Pergamos

312-AD 606. The Licentious Church, (lacking moral restraints) (2:12-17). <u>During this time, the rise of Catholicism and the first pope occurred.</u> Pergamos has the same root word from which we get the English words bigamy and polygamy. It signified that the church had mixed marriages. It is said that Emperor Constantine on Oct. 27, AD 312, saw a vision in the sky and ordered all his army to march through a river to be baptized, thus helping to start the Catholic Church. <u>Their Condemnation</u>: *"I have a few things against thee."* They gave heed to false doctrine, the theology of Balaam. <u>Their sin was joining hands with the world</u>. In other words, I call this worldly compromising. Worldly things got in the way of true Christian living.

4. The Fourth Church -Thyatira

AD 606- AD 1520. The Lax Church (2:18-29).

The Catholic Church gained growth during this time. Popes were Boniface III, Gregory VII, Boniface VIII. This period is known as The Dark Ages. Many Independent fundamental churches would not bow to the Catholic Church. As I mentioned before, <u>the Catholic Church called them Ana-Baptist as a derogatory reference or term</u>. This so-called Papal Church introduced many heathen practices in the following order: baptismal regeneration, justification by works, image worship, priests not to marry, Mariolatry, confessional, purgatory, transubstantiation, indulgences, penance (punishment intended to lead to repentance and sometimes involving the payment of money).

<u>Their Judgment</u>: (2:20-23). It is mentioned that judgment is to come. Those churches allowed Jezebel to teach and seduce them to commit fornication and to eat things sacrificed to idols and, sorry to say, <u>they would not repent</u>. They were told to cast out of this church those who have partook of her sinful activities, including idolatry and unfaithfulness.

CHAPTER 3

<u>5. The Fifth Church – Sardis</u>

AD 1520 –AD 1750. The Dead Church (3:1-6). <u>This is the period of Protestantism</u>. <u>Lutheran Church</u> started with Luther, <u>Presbyterian Church</u> started with Calvin and Knox, <u>Methodist Church</u> started with John Wesley in 1791. <u>The Baptist were already in existence before this period and before the Catholic Church.</u> Technically, Baptist are not Protestant. <u>The word "protestant" means "to protest.</u>" We Baptist did not protest and come out of the Catholic Church. <u>We existed before the Catholic Church. Therefore, Baptists are not Protestants</u>. What I am telling you now is just history. You can easily check it out. Why is the Sardis Church known as being a church that *"liveth and are dead?"* Because this was the Reformation Period. Entire countries became known as Protestant without being born again. I guess they did not believe 2 Cor. 5:17, *"Therefore if any man be in Christ, he is a new creature: old things are passed away; behold, all things are become new."* How about John 3:7 *"Marvel not that I said unto thee, Ye must be born again."*

Sardis was admonished to:
Their works were not perfect before God. (3:2).
They are advised to hold fast and repent. (3:3).
They are also told to remember what they were told.
They are told to watch "for my (Jesus) coming".
They are told that Jesus would suddenly come, so they needed to repent and watch for His coming.

Verses 4-6 state that there are some of these churches who had not caved into the sinful world. (3:4). <u>A challenge to overcome is given in 3:5.</u> "He that overcometh, the same shall be clothed in white raiment; and I will not blot out his name out of the book of life, but I will confess his name before my Father, and before his angels." Verse 6 mentions that they should heed the leading of the Holy Spirit.

6. The Sixth Church

Philadelphia–AD 1750-AD 1900. A Favored Church (3:7-13). (I was born in Philadelphia, but not this one in Revelation). <u>This was the time when missionaries started going around the world.</u> Mission societies, and missionary sending agencies were born. <u>Today the BBFI has over 640 missionaries and the BMA has about that same number.</u> The Church of Philadelphia is complemented for being *"holy and true."* It is recognized as *"he that hath the key of David."* This speaks of Jesus coming from the family of David. The same Jesus who was present in Old Testament times is present now. In other words, <u>this church is a scriptural church.</u> Isa. 9:6: *"For unto us a child is born, unto us a son is given: and the government shall be upon his shoulder: and his name shall be called Wonderful, Counsellor, The mighty God, The everlasting Father, The Prince of Peace."* Rev. 3:7 says they have an open door and no man can shut it. The enemies of Christ cannot shut the door of the church of Jesus Christ. Christ died for the church. Here we see that Jesus loved this church. This is the only church that I find nothing against it mentioned.

7. The Seventh Church – Laodicean Church

AD 1900 – Rapture – This present age - The Lukewarm Church. It became a city of great wealth. In 3:15-16 God said that He knows their works and that this church is neither hot nor cold. That is lukewarm. In fact, He said that He would *"spue thee out of my mouth."* If a person is hot or cold, at least you can tell where they stand. I don't like lukewarm coffee. Ugh! Many churches and Christians are lukewarm today. Years ago, I checked out that word "spue." It means to vomit. So great was His hatred for lukewarmness, that it made him sick. No doubt verse 18 refers to 1 Pet. 1:7. *"That the trial of your faith, being much more precious than of gold that perisheth, though it be tried with fire, might be found unto praise and honour and glory at the appearing of Jesus Christ."* God rebuked them for their attitude of bragging that they were rich and needed nothing. That's like the rich fool in Luke 16:19 who only thought of wanting more riches while not thinking about eternity. There is that famous verse here in Revelation 3:20, *"Behold, I stand at the door, and knock: if any man hear my voice, and open the door, I will come in to him, and will sup with him, and he with me."*

CHAPTER 4

In this chapter, the scene changes from earth to heaven. We studied the 7 churches, but now we turn our attention to the end of the church age. I believe it is not by accident that Revelation, chapter 3 ends with the list of churches, and chapter 4 starts with the call from heaven, "come up hither." I believe that indicates the Rapture. This could happen today. This is when Jesus comes in the clouds to call his people to be with him. We call this THE RAPTURE. When I preached this series on the Revelation, and now as I write this book, the Rapture has not yet happened. Therefore, it is considered prophecy. What is prophecy? Prophecy is history written in advance. There are over 1000 prophecies in the Bible and over 500 have already been fulfilled in exact detail. So, mark it down, the Rapture will happen. The question is, "When, and are you ready?"

I. WHEN AND WHO WILL BE RAPTURED – 4:1

1. The overwhelming preponderance of evidence indicates it will be only the born-again individuals who will be raptured. Notice Dan. 12:2: *"And many of them*

that sleep in the dust of the earth shall awake, some to everlasting life, and some to shame and everlasting contempt. "I think this verse describes the first and last resurrections. Here is the rapture verse.

1 Thes. 4:16-18 16 *"For the Lord himself shall descend from heaven with a shout, with the voice of the archangel, and with the trump of God: and the dead in Christ shall rise first: 17 Then we which are alive and remain shall be caught up together with them in the clouds, to meet the Lord in the air: and so shall we ever be with the Lord."* This will not happen until the church age ends. <u>That could be today! I'm expecting it and I am excited about it.</u>

1 Thes. 4:18 *"Wherefore comfort one another with these words."* That's what I'm looking for. Amen!

II. THE THRONES – Rev. 4:2-4.

1. I agree with most scholars who believe these 24 elders represent the redeemed from the Old and New Testaments. The other thought is that they are representative of the 12 tribes of Israel and the 12 Apostles. I'm not sure and the Bible doesn't say. One sure thing, we will find out. They all are seated on thrones. The saints are reassured throughout scripture that they will reign with Christ. Notice <u>Rev. 20:6</u> – *"Blessed and holy is he that hath part in the first resurrection: on such the second death hath no power, but they shall be priests of God and of Christ, and shall reign with him a thousand years.* "We call that "The Thousand Year Millennial-Reign of Christ."

III. THE CROWNS – vs. 4.

I believe the crown mentioned here is "The Victor's Crown." These have endured humiliation and persecution through the ages. When I think about that, I feel we are about to go through more persecution and discrimination than ever before in the history of the United States. I can almost see the "handwriting on the wall." Already, here in America, children cannot pray in public schools. Prayer in Jesus' name is no longer heard at ball games and mass meetings. Sunday has become Funday instead of Sunday, the Lord's Day.

IV. THE FOUR AND LIVING CREATURES REV. 4:6-8.

1. These are not beasts but living ones. They represent the attributes of the living God. Look at verse 7. *"And the first beast was like a lion, and the second beast like a calf, and the third beast had a face as a man, and the fourth beast was like a flying eagle."* Here is the meaning:

(1) The lion is the well-known symbol of divine majesty and strength.

(2) The ox or calf is also the symbol of strength.

(3) The face of a man indicates intelligence and purpose.

(4) The eagle suggests swiftness in detecting evil and executing judgment.

(5) In verse 8, The six-winged and full of eyes speak of incessant activities and omniscience.

V. THE CHORUS OR PRAISE AND WORSHIP REV. 4:9-11.

Chapter 4 closes with the description of worship in heaven. The four living creatures are described as incessantly worshipping the Lord God Almighty. We should follow their example.

Verse 10 shows us that they cast their crowns before the Lord. This shows that they give all glory to God.

GET READY! JESUS COULD COME TODAY!

THE REVELATION OF JESUS CHRIST SERIES
-SECOND SUNDAY-
CHAPTERS 5,6,7

THE SEALED BOOK, THE 7 SEALED BOOK IS OPENED, THE SEALING OF THE 144,000, AND THE GREAT MULTITUDE OF TRIBULATION SAINTS. REV. 5-7.

INTRO. We finished chapter 4, but 4 and 5 should be together. In chapter 4 the power of God as Creator is emphasized and in chapter 5 the love of God as Redeemer is paramount. We can divide this chapter into 3 divisions: <u>One, the scroll</u>, <u>two, the Savior</u>, <u>three, the song</u>. I've heard that if you can understand the sealed book of chapter 5, you can understand the rest of the Revelation.

Chapter 5

THE SCROLL vs. 1-4.

Rev. 5:1 And I saw in the right hand of him that sat on the throne a book written within and on the backside, sealed with seven seals. 2 And I saw a strong angel proclaiming with a loud voice, Who is worthy to open the book, and to loose the seals thereof? 3 And no man in heaven, nor in earth, neither under the earth, was able to open the book, neither to look thereon. 4 And I wept much, because no man was found worthy to open and to read the book, neither to look thereon.

Think about this: They could not even look at the book, but we hold it in our hands. Now as I take you through chapter 5 of the Revelation, I believe the entire chapter shows the redemptive power of our Lord and Savior Jesus Christ.

Verse 1. The scroll has 7 seals which some call "THE TITLE DEED OF THE REDEEMED." I think it could be called "The Book of Judgment" or "The Book of Destiny." John sees Almighty God sitting on the throne holding in his right hand a 7-sealed scroll indicating perfection since 7 is considered completion. John sees a wonderful sight. He sees Jesus Christ, the Great

Sovereign Savior of the universe. The 24 elders are there. The 4 living creatures are there.

<u>Verse 2.</u> John sees a strong angel with a loud voice crying out, *"Who is worthy to open the book, and to loose the seals thereof?"* <u>This seven-sealed book is a special book, so special that there was only one person who was qualified and strong enough to open the book.</u>

<u>Verse 3.</u> *And no man in heaven, nor in earth, neither under the earth, was able to open the book, neither to look thereon.* Here's the answer. No one was worthy or had the strength to open the scroll. Not even Michael, Gabriel or any of the other archangels volunteered. What a disappointment!

<u>Verse 4.</u> All John could do was weep. He wanted to know what was in the scroll. He had many questions. What about the churches? The future? Even the devil? Heaven?

II. THE SAVIOR – vs. 5-7.

<u>Verse 5.</u> Then John is told to stop weeping. Why? Because <u>Jesus steps fourth</u> as "T*he Lion of the tribe of Juda."* It's Jesus, the triumphant Son of God. Jesus is the central figure in the Book of the Revelation. Jesus is the all-powerful, almighty Son of God. Jesus was the only eligible and strong enough person to open the book.

<u>Verse 6.</u> Now what does John see? The Lion changes to a Lamb with 7 horns and 7 eyes which are the 7 Spirits of God sent forth into the earth. A lion represents bravery and strength. A lamb represents absolute goodness, compassion, and submission. Christ is pictured here as the atoning sacrifice. The 7 horns show He is perfectly

equipped with strength to put down all enemies. The 7 eyes represent the all-seeing eyes of Jesus as He watches over the churches and His people. The destiny of man is in the nail pierced hands of the Lamb that was slain. Which would you like to meet when you turn the corner at some dark street at night? A lion or a lamb? I would rather meet Jesus as the Lamb of God welcoming me into heaven, than a fierce lion saying, *"depart from me; I never knew you"* and be cast into hell.

Verse 7. *And he came and took the book out of the right hand of him that sat upon the throne.* That word *"took,"* I heard is in the dramatic perfect tense representing immediate and determined finality when the Glorified Redeemer took the book. He took it with determination and resolve. As a lion of the tribe of Judah, He has all power. Jesus said, *"All power is given unto me in heaven and in earth."* Jesus is God in the flesh, the Almighty God which means He has "All power."

III. THE SONG – vs. 8-14.

The rest of Chapter 5 is full of supreme praise culminating in song. Here the scene suddenly erupts into a glorious chorus. The music, the song, the praise will explode into enthusiastic praise and honor to our Savior who alone was worthy enough and had power enough to take the book and open it to reveal God's final plan for planet earth and the eternal heaven. Listen to the praise and worship given to Jesus as He steps forth. Notice Rev. 5:11-12: 11 *And I beheld, and I heard the voice of many angels round about the throne and the beasts and the elders: and the number of them was ten thousand times ten thousand, and thousands of thousands; 12 Saying with a loud voice, Worthy is the Lamb that was slain to receive power, and riches, and wisdom, and strength, and honor, and glory, and blessing.*

How many is ten thousand times ten thousand, and thousands of thousands? Ten thousand times ten thousand would be a hundred million and add to these "thousands of thousands." That is at least two thousand times two thousand or a minimum of four million more. <u>So there are at least 104 million angels</u>. What a scene! But that is not the total number of God's angels. Hebrews 12:22, describes an *"innumerable company of angels"* that are too great to count.

CHAPTER 6

Now we come to the nitty-gritty part of the Revelation, the central messages of the Revelation. <u>It begins in chapter 6, verse 1 and continues through chapter 19, verse 6. These chapters deal with the Seven-Year Tribulation Period.</u> To understand dates and times, remember that the word "weeks" actually means "sevens." Allow me to read Daniel 9:20-27. 20 *"And whiles I was speaking, and praying, and confessing my sin and the sin of my people Israel, and presenting my supplication before the LORD my God for the holy mountain of my God; 21 Yea, whiles I was speaking in prayer, even the man Gabriel, whom I had seen in the vision at the beginning, being caused to fly swiftly, touched me about the time of the evening oblation. 22 And he informed me, and talked with me, and said, O Daniel, I am now come forth to give thee skill and understanding. 23 At the beginning of thy supplications the commandment came forth, and I am come to shew thee; for thou art greatly beloved: therefore understand the matter, and consider the vision. 24 Seventy weeks are determined upon thy people* *and upon thy holy city, to finish the transgression, and to make an end of sins, and to make reconciliation for iniquity, and to bring in everlasting righteousness, and to seal up the vision and prophecy, and to anoint the most Holy. 25 Know therefore and understand, that <u>from the going forth of the commandment to restore and to build Jerusalem unto the Messiah the Prince shall be seven weeks, and threescore and two weeks</u>: the street shall be built again, and the wall, even in troublous times. 26 And after threescore and two weeks shall Messiah be cut off, but not for himself: and the people of the prince that shall come shall destroy the city and the sanctuary; and the end thereof shall be with a flood, and unto the end of the war desolations are determined. 27 And he shall confirm the covenant with many for one week: and in the midst of the week he shall cause the sacrifice and the oblation to cease, and for the overspreading of abominations he shall make it desolate, even until the consummation, and that determined shall be poured upon the desolate.* Here is the explanation for all that. The Lord revealed to Daniel that the future of the nation of Israel from the decree to rebuild the city of Jerusalem would be divided into seventy "sevens" of years; seventy "seven-year periods." <u>The decree to rebuild Jerusalem was proclaimed by Artaxerxes and given to Nehemiah in 445 BC.</u> Daniel was told in his vision that 69 of the 70 weeks would extend from the decree to rebuild the city unto the Jew's final rejection of their Messiah. <u>From the date that Artaxerxes issued his decree until the date that Jesus Christ made His triumphal entrance into Jerusalem on Palm Sunday was 483 years. They counted a year as 360</u>

days. Therefore 69 years of Daniel's prophecy have been fulfilled. What about the 70th week? That 70th week is the Tribulation Period of 7 years.

THE 7 SEALS OPENED – 4 BEASTS
THE LAMB OF GOD (JESUS) WORSHIPPED.

Try to envision the sight as we see the Lamb open the first seal in a 7-sealed book. The last few verses in chapter 5 set the scene here. Imagine at least 104 million angels praising the Lord, the Lamb of God and singing, 11 *"And I beheld, and I heard the voice of many angels round about the throne and the beasts and the elders: and the number of them was ten thousand times ten thousand, and thousands of thousands;* 12 *Saying with a loud voice, Worthy is the Lamb that was slain to receive power, and riches, and wisdom, and strength, and honour, and glory, and blessing.* 13 *And every creature which is in heaven, and on the earth, and under the earth, and such as are in the sea, and all that are in them, heard I saying, Blessing, and honor, and glory, and power, be unto him that sitteth upon the throne, and unto the Lamb for ever and ever.* 14 *And the four beasts* (5:6) *said, Amen. And the four and twenty elders fell down and worshipped him that liveth for ever and ever."* WOW! Now we enter the most horrible part of the Tribulation. The unimaginable 7 Seal Judgments, 7 Trumpet Judgments, and 7 Vial or Bowl Judgments.

II. THE RIDER ON THE WHITE HORSE-ANTI-CHRIST Rev. 6:1-2

FIRST SEAL OPENED

This is not Jesus. Now we come to the horrible 7 seals. I know you will think these 7 seals are extremely horrible and devastating but wait till we come to the 7 trumpets and especially the 7 bowls.

The one on the white horse here in chapter 6 is not Jesus. Rev. 6 and Rev. 19 both have riders on white horses. This one in chapter 6 can only be the Anti-Christ. He counterfeits the real Christ who will ride a white horse in Chapter 19. I am certain the one that Christ rides is a great white stallion. Here Christ is the one who opens this first seal. When it is opened, the noise of thunder is heard. I believe this thunder indicated impending catastrophe and is an attention-getter. If God uses thunder for judgment, it must not be just ordinary thunder, but supernatural thunder, ear-piercing thunder.

(vs. 1). The Anti-Christ will be a superman with great powers. He will do great things that causes the whole world to accept him and believe he is the Christ. He will be very persuasive with his smooth appealing speech. There is a striking contrast between this rider and the one in 19:11-15 which we will get to later in our series. There have been many world rulers in human history: (Pharaoh, Belshazzar, Alexander the Great, Julius Caesar, Napoleon, Adolph Hitler, Stalin, etc.) but none will surpass the brutality and power of the one on this white horse, the Anti-Christ. Much can be said about this rider. He comes with a bow and no arrows showing that he has the answer for world peace.

III. THE RIDER ON THE RED HORSE. 6:3-4

SECOND SEAL OPENED

Rev. 6:3 *And when he had opened the second seal, I heard the second beast say, Come and see. 4 And there went out another horse that was red: and power was given to him that sat thereon to take peace from the earth, and that they should kill one another: and there was given unto him a great sword.* Now the Lamb (Jesus) opens the second seal, and a red horse appears. Red is the color of blood which symbolizes bloodshed, violence, killings, and war. While this rider pretends to bring peace, devastation and destruction follow. It's like the so-called "peaceful demonstrations" that turn out everything but peaceful. The sword he carries is a *GREAT sword*.

THIRD SEAL OPENED

IV. THE RIDER ON THE BLACK HORSE 6:5-6.

When this seal is opened, the rider on this black horse has a pair of balances in his hand. This introduces world-wide FAMINE, worse than ever before in history. Food will be so expensive that it will take a full day's wages to buy a measure of wheat or three measures of barley. In today's money it would amount to $200.00 for a bushel of wheat, but there won't be much of it. People will have to buy barley, a food for horses. Can you imagine the panic that causes mass riots, looting and even murder? Sorry to say, "We in America know what rioting is all about. People riot, destroy innocent people's property over the government requirement of wearing a mask. This Corona virus has caused people to revolt and cause violence. <u>Without proper food, disease and sickness will increase</u>. Inflation will skyrocket. The Antichrist's numerical program will replace gold, silver, and money. Notice Ezek. 7:19. *They shall cast their silver in the streets, and their gold shall be removed: their silver and their gold shall not be able to deliver them in the day of the wrath of the LORD: they shall not satisfy their souls, neither fill their bowels: because it is the stumbling block of their iniquity.*

Here is some FLASH NEWS. On Sunday, February 14th, 2021, I heard on the news that we are advised to conserve on food because it will get scarce. Also, many cities in Missouri are running out of gas, so we are to use gas sparingly. Even toilet paper has been rationed. These things are going on now as I write this. It will be worse when the Antichrist takes over. Friends, the Covid-19 pandemic is a prelude to what will take place during the Tribulation Period. There is but one way to prepare. Come to Jesus now and ask Him to come into your heart and save you. I believe that real soon God will look at His Son Jesus and say, "It's time. Go get my children and bring them home."

THE FOURTH SEAL OPENED - PALE = DEATH

V. THE RIDER ON THE PALE HORSE – 6:7-8.

Look at Rev. 6:7-8. *7 And when he had opened the fourth seal, I heard the voice of the fourth beast say,*

Come and see. 8 And I looked, and behold a pale horse: and his name that sat on him was Death, and Hell followed with him. And power was given unto them over the fourth part of the earth, to kill with sword, and with hunger, and with death, and with the beasts of the earth. This rider will be more ferocious than the first three. Pale denotes a leprous corpse, putrefying flesh. The war, famine and bloodshed will result in one-fourth of the people in the world dying. The world population is 8 billion now. That means $1/4^{th}$ would be 2 billion people. That's the population of China, America, Russia and Germany combined. Think about it…$1/4^{th}$ of the population dying. More would have died, but due to the 144,000 Jewish evangelists preaching, only ¼ of the world died. Isaiah 5:14 tells us that hell had to enlarge itself. Did you know that hell was not made for humans? It was made for the devil and his angels. Notice Mat. 25:41. *Then shall he say also unto them on the left hand, Depart from me, ye cursed, into everlasting fire, prepared for the devil and his angels.* People became so sinful that hell had to enlarge itself. We read about the WHITE HORSE with the antichrist coming on the scene. Then the RED HORSE symbolizing bloodshed, violence, killings, and war. Next was the BLACK HORSE that causes worldwide famine. The last one was the PALE HORSE of death when one-fourth of the world dies. If you are saved, you don't have to be concerned about all that. However, your unsaved friends will be there to suffer. You had better warn them now.

THE FIFTH SEAL OPENED 6:9-11
VI. THE CRY FOR VENGEANCE

John SEES the SOULS of the martyrs. They are the Tribulation martyrs. During the tribulation time they are killed for the *"Word of their testimony, and who love not their lives unto the death."* (Rev. 12:11). During this time there will still be

the preaching of the Gospel. *"And the Gospel of the Kingdom shall be preached in all the world for a witness unto all nations; and then shall the end come."* (Matt. 24:14). Of course, the Anti-Christ doesn't like that so *"Great persecution"* results. These *"souls under the altar"* were given white robes. They cried out for vengeance. Rev. 6:10 says, *"And they cried with a loud voice, saying, how long, O Lord, holy and true, dost thou not judge and avenge our blood on them that dwell on the earth?"* During this terrible time many will be saved, but they will suffer much. We'll get into that study in a future message. They will have to be saved the same way we get saved today, by trusting in the shed blood of Jesus Christ. We learn from this that there is no such thing as "soul sleep." Once they are saved and martyred, their soul goes immediately to be with the Lord (2 Cor. 5:8). *We are confident, I say, and willing rather to be absent from the body, and to be present with the Lord.* When a person dies, their soul and spirit immediately go to be with the Lord, but their bodies are buried to be raised and united with the soul at the resurrection. One sure thing, being in spirit form does not mean unconsciousness. Spirits move, talk, cry, and even wear white robes. These martyrs cry out for vengeance. They went through great persecution. Satan may be having his heyday now, but God will take care of him. God in heaven sits on His throne and laughs at those who oppose Him (Psalm 2:4). *He that sitteth in the heavens shall laugh: the Lord shall have them in derision.*

VII.

THE SIXTH SEAL OPENED. 6:12-17.

When this 6th seal is opened, things happen. There will be an *EARTHQUAKE, THE SUN BLACKENED, THE MOON APPEARS AS RED AS BLOOD, STARS (METEORS) RAIN ON THE EARTH, MOUNTAINS AND ISLANDS MOVE OUT OF PLACE.* Let's consider these events.

(1) EARTHQUAKE – 6:12. It is called a *"great" earthquake*. Have you ever experienced an earthquake? While living in Japan I have experienced several. The world has had many earthquakes, some with a magnitude of 9.5. America has had 175 major earthquakes since 1700. Even today (June 10th, 2022), 121 earthquakes have been reported in the last 24 hours in the USA. I'm sure they were very light, but still they were reported. Believe me, an earthquake will get your attention. I really believe this earthquake that happens when the 6th seal opens is literal. I understand the Greek word for "great" in this instance is "violent." It will be worse than any the world has experienced.

(2) *SUN BECOMES BLACK AS SACKCLOTH* – 6:12.

What is "sackcloth"? I checked it out and discovered it is "a coarsely woven fabric, usually made of goat's hair.

"This is also foretold by Isaiah in 50:3 – *"I clothe the heavens with blackness, and I make sackcloth their covering."* Remember the darkness that covered the earth when Jesus was hanging on the cross in Luke 2:44-45? One day when I was sitting at home, suddenly a cloud covered the sun, and it became almost as dark as night. That was kind of scary. This blackness in Revelation will be so black that you can feel it. Remember the darkness when Moses caused that to happen in Egypt when Pharaoh would not let the Jews leave? It became so dark that they could not do anything for 3 days. They couldn't see each other. This one in the Revelation will be far worse.

(3) THE MOON BECOMES LIKE BLOOD RED – 6:12. I have never seen a moon as red as blood. Here it is not real blood, but *AS blood*. No wonder men's hearts will fail them, and fear will be over all the earth. Again, remember the darkness when Moses caused that to happen in Egypt when Pharaoh would not let the Jews leave? If it happened then, it could happen again.

(4) THE STARS FALL FROM HEAVEN – 6:13 This means not just one or two stars, but many like figs fall from trees when the wind blows. I can't imagine the destruction that will cause. On Nov.13, 1833 a similar thing happened. Some thought it was the end of the world. Here's what was reported at that time. "Fiery balls, as luminous and almost as numerous as the stars themselves, came darting after each other from the sky with glorious streaks of light trailing each meteor in its train!" God can and will make it happen again. These are scary things. I'm glad I'm saved and will be in heaven

when that happens.

(5) THE HEAVEN DEPARTS AS A SCROLL – 6:14. I don't know how to describe this, but it must be powerful since every mountain and island is moved out of their places. One commentary says, "It is like a scroll that is opened, but it suddenly rolls up and closes with a snap."

(6) PEOPLE HIDE THEMSELVES IN CAVES – 6:15-17. Rev 6:15 15 *And the kings of the earth, and the great men, and the rich men, and the chief captains, and the mighty men, and every bondman, and every free man, hid themselves in the dens and in the rocks of the mountains;* 16 *And said to the mountains and rocks, Fall on us, and hide us from the face of him that sitteth on the throne, and from the wrath of the Lamb:* 17 *For the great day of his wrath is come; and who shall be able to stand?* So great is the fear that kings, rich and poor, military soldiers, strong men, and everyone else try to hide in the dens in the mountains. <u>They even cry to the mountains to fall on them. Their fear is so great, they want to die.</u> There will be no place to hide. Joel 2:10 has something to say about this. *The earth shall quake before them; the heavens shall tremble: the sun and the moon shall be dark, and the stars shall withdraw their shining.* I am not trying to scare you if you are not saved, but actually, I would rather scare people into heaven than to sugar-coat the Word of God and lure them into hell.

CHAPTER 7

I. THOSE SAVED DURING THE TRIBULATION – (AN INTERLUDE)

An explanation of what happens to those saved during the Tribulation is the purpose of chapter 7. God shows how He protects those saved during this terrible time. However, the saved who will not compromise their faith will suffer persecution and death. Rev. 7:1-8 tells of the 144,000 Jewish evangelists sealed. Let's look more closely at this event. God shows how He holds back four angels from hurting the earth, including the sea and trees until 144,000 Jewish evangelists from the 12 tribes of Israel are sealed. There will be many who are saved who will not compromise their faith and will suffer persecution and death.

II. THE FOUR ANGELS AND 144,000 APPEAR DURING THE TRIBULATION – 7:1-8

Four angels appear standing at the *"four corners of the earth."* They are holding back the four winds of judgment. Then we see 144,000 Jewish evangelists sealed in their foreheads and are protected as they go about preaching. These 144,000 Jewish evangelists, I believe were sent by God so that many people would hear the message of salvation and get saved. <u>The 144,000 consisted of 12,000 from the 12 tribes of Israel.</u> Those 12 tribes were Juda, Reuben, Gad, Aser, Nephalim, Manasses, Simeon, Levi, Issachar, Zebulon, Joseph, and Benjamin. Of the original 12 tribes, Dan and Ephraim are not included. Why? Probably because they were guilty of going into idolatry (Jud. 18:1, 1Kings11:26 and Hosea 4.) Levi and Manasseh take their place. However, they are included in the Millennial Temple (Ezek. 48). <u>These 144,000 will be supernaturally protected during the tribulation.</u>

III. THE GREAT MULTITUDE SAVED DURING THE TRIBULATION – 7:9-17.

We see here *"After this,"* after what? After the 144,000 are sealed. We also see "a great number saved." Yes, people will hear the Gospel and multitudes will be saved. <u>Those who are saved will be dressed in white robes</u>. They are happy because they survived the first 6 seals. However, many who hear the Gospel and reject it, will have no chance to be saved. <u>It is noteworthy to notice that no saved will enter the Tribulation.</u> Unsaved people will hear the 144,000 and many will be saved by trusting in the shed blood of Jesus Christ. Most of these will be martyred. What a beautiful scene! 11 *And all the angels stood round about the throne, and about the elders and the four beasts, and fell before the throne on their faces, and worshipped God, 12 Saying, Amen: Blessing, and glory, and wisdom, and thanksgiving, and honour, and power, and might, be unto our God for ever and ever. Amen.* Sad to say, many who hear the Gospel and reject it, will have no chance to be saved. We who are saved now, need not worry. We will already be in heaven.

My advice: Don't take a chance and put off salvation. The door is open now, but the day is coming when it will cost you your life to get saved.

WE WHO ARE SAVED WON'T BE THERE

THE REVELATION OF JESUS CHRIST SERIES
THIRD SUNDAY
CHAPTERS 8, 9,10
THE SEALED BOOK, THE 7 SEALED BOOK IS OPEN, SILENCE IN HEAVEN, 7TH SEAL OPENED, THE 7 TRUMPETS SOUND.

INTRO. We have studied the first 6 seals of the 7-sealed book. Now the 7th seal is opened and there is silence in Heaven for one-half hour and the 7 trumpets begin to sound.

CHAPTER 8

THE SEVENTH SEAL

I. SILENCE IN HEAVEN FOR ONE-HALF HOUR. 8:1

This is an awesome, overwhelming silence. Nothing is moving in heaven. Having experienced the devastation of the first 6 seals and perhaps knowing what is coming, there is a weird silence. This could be called "The calm before the storm." Then also, God knew they needed a break.

II. THE SEVEN TRUMPETS GIVEN TO 7 ANGELS. 8:2

Trumpets in the Word of God often sound the alarm for judgment to come. I like trumpets. I play the trumpet, but the trumpets in The Book of The Revelation will not be playing march music like I played in the Air Force marching band. The Revelation trumpets will be sounding an alarm and a warning. Num.10:9 tells us, *"And if ye go to war in your land against the enemy that oppresseth you, then ye shall blow an alarm with the trumpets; and ye shall be remembered before the LORD your God, and ye shall be saved from your enemies."*

III. THE PRAYERS OF THE SAINTS. 8:3-5

Before the 7 trumpets sound, an angel was given a golden censer. Incense was given to him which he was to offer with the prayers of the saints. He filled the censer with fire from the altar and threw it to the earth. Then voices, lightnings, thunder and an earthquake took place.

IV. THE SEVEN ANGELS PREPARED TO SOUND. 8:7-10:7

THE FIRST TRUMPET SOUNDED – REV. 8:7.

This hail, fire and blood are literal. It reminds me of the 7th plague that fell upon Egypt. A third part of the trees were burned up. All green grass was burned up. What will happen to the cattle and sheep that depend on grass? With fruit trees gone, what will people do? Perhaps this is what Joel was explaining in Joel 1:18-20. *18 How do the beasts groan! The herds of cattle are perplexed, because they have no pasture; yea, the flocks of sheep are made desolate. 19 O LORD, to thee will I cry: for the fire hath devoured the pastures of the wilderness, and the flame hath burned all the trees of the field. 20 The beasts of the field cry also unto thee: for the rivers of waters are dried up, and the fire hath devoured the pastures of the wilderness.*

THE SECOND TRUMPET SOUNDED – 8:8.

When this second angel sounds the trumpet, the judgment which follows is so great, it is like a great mountain. However, the fire that was cast into the sea and a third part of the sea became blood is literal. A third part of all creatures in the sea died and a third part of all ships were destroyed. That is all literal. I think this will get the attention of all living at that time.

THE THIRD TRUMPET SOUNDED – 8:10.

When this third angel sounds the trumpet, a great burning star falls from heaven. This star is literal. Maybe a great meteor. It was a ball of fire that fell on a third part of the rivers. The rivers became bitter because this star was wormwood. The English rendering "wormwood" refers to the dark green oil produced by the plant, which was used to kill intestinal worms. Many die from this bitter wormwood. Wow!

THE FOURTH TRUMPET SOUNDED – 8:12.

This fourth trumpet judgment has to do with the earth's light – the sun, moon, and stars. Coincidental or not, I don't know, but it was the fourth day that God said, *"Let there be lights in the firmament of heaven."* (Gen. 1:14). I get an eerie feeling when the clouds cover the sun in the middle of the day. The God who created the lights can extinguish them at his will. What happens is up to your imagination. But the worst is yet to come. This fourth angel has another angel with him. He flies through heaven crying *"WOE, WOE, WOE!"* What's that all about? <u>I have an idea now in the middle of the Tribulation,</u> this angel is letting us know that the last half will be far worse than the first half. <u>The last half of the Tribulation will be the most horrible time the earth has</u>

ever experienced. Matt. 24:21 describes the last 3 ½ years as *"The Great Tribulation."* I notice that the first 4 trumpet judgments take up 1 or 2 verses each, but the 5th Trumpet Judgment takes up 12 verses and the 6th Trumpet Judgment takes up 9 verses. Do you get the idea?

CHAPTER 9

FIRST WOE

THE FIFTH TRUMPET JUDGMENT   REV 9:1-12.

We now come to the fifth trumpet. Having read about this fifth trumpet a number of times, I feel like crying out "WOE, WOE, WOE," since I know what happens. Here a star falls from heaven unto the earth. That star that falls from heaven is not a literal star since verse one says, *"I saw a star fall from heaven unto the earth: and to him was given the key to the bottomless pit."* Not *"it,"* but *"him."* A person! Perhaps an angel acting for Christ. He is "given the key to the bottomless pit." When He opens it, out come smoke so dense that it obliterates the light from the sun. Then here come the locusts. What are locusts? I think locusts are locusts. They certainly were literal locusts back when there was a plague of locusts in Moses' day. Why not literal now? I know that some scholars think they are demons from the bottomless pit in the form of locusts. They may be right, but I can't say. Far be it for me to dispute those who believe locust are not locust. Listen to the description of them in 9:3-11. They had power like scorpions. They were not interested in the grass, trees, etc., but only in stinging those who did not have the seal of God in their foreheads. They did not kill, but they tormented men for five months. Their shape was like horses prepared for battle. On their heads were crowns like gold. Their faces were as the faces of men. Their hair as the hair of woman, and their teeth were as the teeth of lions. They had breastplates of iron and their wings had the sound of many chariots. In other words, they were noisy. They had a king over them whose name was Abaddon in Hebrew meaning destruction and Apollyon meaning Destroyer.

During this horrible painful time, people will seek death. They will try to kill themselves but they won't be able to do that. Rev 9:6 *And in those days shall men seek death, and shall not find it; and shall desire to die, and death shall flee from them.* Have you ever been in pain that you wished you could die? No wonder that verse 12 says, *"One woe is past; behold, there come two woes more hereafter."*

THE SIXTH TRUMPET   REV. 9:13-21

When this sixth angel sounds the trumpet, a voice from the four horns of the golden altar gives the order to the sixth angel who had a trumpet to loose the four angels that are bound in the great river Euphrates. The Euphrates is mentioned 21 times in the Bible, but the first time in Revelation. This river is extremely important, and I will get into that soon. The four horns of the golden altar are where the guilty sinner could cling for mercy. Could this be a cry for vengeance?

(I don't know how many times I had to stop as I was studying this sixth trumpet angel because it was so overwhelming). All I could do was to put my hands on my head and internally cry out, "Lord, Lord, Lord." I couldn't help thinking, "Will people be running away from destruction while crying out My God, My God, My God like I saw people running from the falling buildings which we remember as 911, or Sept. 11, 2021.

What we have here I believe to be the preparation for the Battle of Armageddon that won't happen until the end of the Tribulation recorded in chapter 16. These 4 angels are part of the angels which were cast out of heaven with Satan.

Right now, I believe they are there waiting to be released. The area of the Euphrates River is where the Tower of Babel stood, where the first murder was committed, the garden of Eden was there, the worship of demons started there.

Let's take a close look at Rev. 9:15-21. Horrible destruction is caused by these fallen angels. An army of 200,000,000 assemble. The horses they ride are described as having heads like lions from which fire, smoke and brimstone came. I know some of you theologians are wondering about this. Is this when the Battle of Armageddon occurs? No, it is not. The Battle of Armageddon is mentioned here and in Chapters 9,16 and 19. A little is mentioned about it each time. Here in chapter 9, verse 18 we read that a third part of men were destroyed. Don't forget that this is an additional one third since back in chapter 6 one fourth died when the pale horse of death appeared. Here in chapter 9, there are still 6 billion people left, but a third part of men will die. This is not the actual Battle of Armageddon here in Rev. 9

since that doesn't happen in the middle of the Tribulation, but at the end. Think of living during that time being stung with these monster "horses" of hell. Now think of this...verses 20-21 says, 20 *"And the rest of the men which were not killed by these plagues yet repented not of the works of their hands, that they should not worship devils, and idols of gold, and silver, and brass, and stone, and of wood: which neither can see, nor hear, nor walk:* 21 *Neither repented they of their murders, nor of their sorceries, nor of their fornication, nor of their thefts.* As a missionary to Japan, I saw thousands at the Buddhist's temples and Shinto shrines worshiping idols made by men's hands. I felt so sorry for them. When possible, I gave them tracts about our true God who created heaven and earth. Of course, these tracts invited them to receive Jesus as their Savior.

CHAPTER 10

You would expect to hear about the 7th trumpet here, but another interlude takes place. The 7th trumpet doesn't appear until 11:14-15 when the third WOE and the 7th trumpet sounds. This interlude actually has two parts. Part one covers chapter 10 and part two chapter 11:1-13. I call this interlude "the calm before the storm."

A SUMMARY OF THE FIRST PART OF THIS INTERLUDE – 10:1-10

He is called "The Mighty Angel" because He is Jesus Christ. *For by him were all things created, that are in heaven, and that are in earth, visible and invisible, whether they be thrones, or dominions, or principalities, or powers: all things were created by him, and for him:* (Col. 1:16). Jesus sometimes appeared in the O.T. as an angel. Jesus appeared as an angel in Rev. 7:2-3, 8:5 and now in 10:1.

What is the significance of Jesus standing with His right foot upon the sea and His left foot on land in verse 2? I believe He was demonstrating how that He is the creator of the entire world, and the day is coming when

He will be the King of kings and Lord of lords. The earth and the sea are his since He is the creator. <u>As He was standing there He cried with a loud voice like a lion. Then seven thunders uttered their voices.</u> God told John not to write about those seven thunders. I wonder what that is all about. If the Bible is silent about that, far be it for me to try to explain it. It might be so overwhelming that we wouldn't be able to handle such information. Then the angel, that is Jesus, lifted his hand to heaven and swore to Almighty God that time shall be no more. He is saying that the end is coming, and the mystery of God would be finished as He had declared to his servants, the prophets.

THE LITTLE BOOK 10:8-11

Then John is told to take a little book that is in the hand of the angel *"which standeth upon the sea and upon the earth."* He is told to eat the book. I think this is part of the Word of God. <u>When he does, he finds it is sweet as honey, but is bitter in his belly. When he eats this little book, I believe the honey part is the good news that anyone can be saved, but the bitter part is *"he that believeth not shall be damned."* The honey part is *"For God so loved the world."* The bitter part is *"For all have sinned."*</u>

If you are lost today, you must suffer the bitter end, but if you are saved today, your future will be sweet as honey.

REMEMBER THIS! WE WHO ARE SAVED WON'T BE THERE!

THE REVELATION OF JESUS CHRIST SERIES
FOURTH SUNDAY
CHAPTERS 11, 12, 13

CHAPTER 11 TRIBULATION WITNESSES, 42 MONTHS, 1260 DAYS, 3RD WOE, 7TH TRUMPET
CHAPTER 12 WOMAN WITH MAN CHILD, RED DRAGON, WOMAN IN WILDERNESS, TIME, TIME AND HALF A TIME. CHAPTER 13 HEADED BEAST, WORLD GOVERNMENT, 42 MONTHS, LAMB/DRAGON, FALSE PROPHET.

INTRO. In Chapter 10 we studied about the Mighty Angel and about the Little Book. Now we come to the 2nd half of the interlude between the 6th and 7th seals. The main theme of this interlude is the 2 witnesses. Who are they and what do they do?

CHAPTER 11

I. THE TEMPLE OF GOD VS. 1,2.

Verses 1 and 2 are interesting. It has to do with John being given a reed or measuring stick. An angel told John to measure the temple of God. There have been three temples built.

1. First, the Temple planned by David and built by Solomon and destroyed by Nebuchadnezzar.

2. Second, the Temple built by Ezra, Nehemiah and Zerubbabel which was destroyed by Antiochus Epiphanes.

3. Third, Herod's Temple which was there when Jesus walked this earth. It was destroyed by Titus in AD 70.

The Mosque of Omar is in the place where God's temple should be today. It is sacred to the Mohammedans. I believe that temple will be taken down and the Temple of God will be built there. A covenant will be made between the Jews and the antichrist. That's the temple that John is told to measure. When God tells someone to measure something, He is saying that it belongs to Him. Zechariah 2 and Ezekiel 40 have examples.

II. THE TWO WITNESSES VS. 3-14.

1. Who are they? <u>This has always been a friendly disagreement</u>. I am quite sure that one of them is Elijah. Many think the other one is Moses. I also believe it will be Moses and Elijah because they appeared with Jesus on the Mount of Transfiguration (Mark 9:4). Some believe it will be Elijah and Enoch because they did not die. I don't know! <u>When we get to heaven, we will find out. That's good enough for me.</u>

2. When will they prophesy? 11:3-5 - These two witnesses' prophesy for 1260 days or 3 ½ years during the last half of the Tribulation.

3. Their power. 11:6 – They can cause it to rain or not rain. They have power to turn the rivers into blood and to smite the earth with plagues.

4. How they are protected? 11:5 – No one can hurt them until they finish what God gave them to do at the end of 1260 days. Those who try to kill them will experience fire spewing out of their mouths. They learn quickly not to mess with God's witnesses. I think it is a dangerous thing to hurt God's servants even today.

5. They experience persecution - 7-10 – When their testimony is ended (and not before) the beast that come out of the Abyss (the antichrist), will make war on them. <u>Really? The enemies of Christ need a full blast war to fight just two people? The Anti-Christ will kill them and leave their bodies in the streets of Jerusalem for 3 ½ days. The people will rejoice and send gifts to celebrate their death.</u> The rejoicing will end when after 3 ½ days when God's spirit enters them, and they stand up. A voice from heaven will call them to *"come up hither."*

6. The great earthquake - 11:13. Listen to what comes next.

"And the same hour was there a great earthquake, and the tenth part of the city fell, and in the earthquake were slain of men seven thousand: and the remnant were affrighted, and gave glory to the God of heaven" (11:13). They saw the 2 witnesses come back to life and became frightened. <u>God got their attention.</u> Seven thousand people died.

<u>I think the covid-19 virus of 2020-2021 was a wake up call for America and the world to repent and turn to God before it is to late.</u> Due to the fact that we were forced to take the Covid shots, I feel we may already be programed to take the 666 mark during the Tribulation Period, but we Christians living today won't be there then. Praise the Lord for that. We had better warn our unsaved friends and family members to get saved now.

III. THE THIRD WOE, THE 7TH TRUMPET AND THE ANNOUNCEMENT OF FUTURE EVENTS – 11:15-19.

<u>Verse 14 tells us that the 2nd and 3rd "woes" are past, but now the 7th trumpet sounds.</u> The other 2 WOES were bad enough but watch out for the 7th trumpet. In the case of the 7 seals and 7 trumpets, immediate judgment fell on the earth, <u>but in the case of the 7th trumpet, we are caused to wait before we hear the 7th trumpet sound and the 7 vials or 7 bowls are poured on earth.</u> We need to hear about this so that we might understand what follows. My guess is that John was told to insert this information between the trumpets and the vials so the reader could take a break after hearing of the destruction caused by the

seals and trumpets. That's just my guess.

A preview of what is to come – Rev. 11:15 – The cry is heard, *"The kingdoms of this world are become the kingdoms of our Lord, and of his Christ; and he shall reign for ever and ever."* <u>Actually, this had not happened yet, but those who were saying these things considered it as something that had happened.</u> However, this was something that was anticipated. They were celebrating the fact that Jesus had already come to set up his kingdom. There was a great shout of joy. They were singing *"and He shall reign for ever and ever."* When all of this happens in the future, all people will bow to the One who will reign forever and ever. Hallelujah! Amen!

The four and 20 elders fall upon their faces before God in anxious anticipation of what is to come – Rev. 11:16-18. <u>Some people claim these are representative of the Old and New Testament saints</u>. I must admit that <u>I do not know</u>. The Word of God does not say a lot about them other than in (11:16,17). 16 *And the four and twenty elders, which sat before God on their seats, fell upon their faces, and worshipped God,* 17 *Saying, We give thee thanks, O Lord God Almighty, which art, and wast, and art to come; because thou hast taken to thee thy great power, and hast reigned.* They gave all the glory to God Almighty. They know firsthand that Satan has been the god of this world system (2 Cor. 4:4). They know that the nations of this world have been under his control (Mat. 6:8,9). But now, they see the end and they rejoice as though it was already finished. They are worshipping God in happy anticipation. The nations were angry – 18-19. Listen to what vs. 18 says, <u>*"And the nations were*</u>

angry, and thy wrath is come, and the time of the dead, that they should be judged, and that thou shouldest give reward unto thy servants the prophets, and to the saints, and them that fear thy name, small and great; and shouldest destroy them which destroy the earth." <u>Really? Well, I say, "Go ahead, you nations, and see what your anger will do against the One and only Almighty God."</u> Now listen to God's response in verse 19: *"and the temple of God was opened in heaven, and there was seen in his temple the ark of the testament: and there were lightnings, and voices, and thunderings, and an earthquake, and great hail."* Go with what the Bible says, plus nothing and minus nothing. *When it says there were lightnings, and voices, thunderings and an earthquake, and great hail,* I BELIEVE IT!

CHAPTER 12

LAST HALF OF THE TRIBULATION PERIOD.
Now we leave the parenthesis or interlude between the sixth and seventh trumpets and actually continue into the last half of the seven-year tribulation period. We do not see what happens when the seven vials or bowls are blown until the 16th chapter.

In this chapter we will see seven important events.
1. THE (WONDER) SIGN OF THE WOMAN – VS. 1
2. THE GREAT RED DRAGON – VS. 3-11
3. WAR IN HEAVEN – VS. 7-9
4. THE VICTORIOUS CRY FROM HEAVEN – VS. 10-11
5. GREAT WRATH – VS. 12-13
6. THE WINGS OF A GREAT EAGLE – VS. 14-17
7. HOW GOD PROTECTS ISRAEL – VS. 15-17

I. THE WONDER OR SIGN OF THE WOMAN WHO IS A PICTURE OF ISRAEL – 12:1.
Rev. 12:1 *And there appeared a great wonder in*

heaven; a woman clothed with the sun, and the moon under her feet, and upon her head a crown of twelve stars: The proof of this is found in Gen. 37:9-10. *And he dreamed yet another dream, and told it his brethren, and said, Behold, I have dreamed a dream more; and behold, the sun and the moon and the eleven stars (Joseph being the 12th star) made obeisance to me. 10 And he told it to his father, and to his brethren: and his father rebuked him, and said unto him, What is this dream that thou hast dreamed? Shall I and thy mother and thy brethren indeed come to bow down ourselves to thee to the earth?* <u>Clearly the woman clothed with the sun and wearing a crown of exactly 12 stars is Israel.</u>

Now in 12:2, *"And she being with child, traveling in birth, and pained to be delivered"* <u>is the mother, Israel, bringing forth a man-child who is none other than the Lord Jesus.</u> Christ, in His flesh, came forth from Israel; and, at this point, Christ's adversary, Satan, the one who rebelled centuries ago against the authority of God is right now about to take another blow.

II. THE GREAT RED DRAGON – VS. 3-11

Without a doubt, this *"Great Red Dragon"* is Satan. Verse 9 makes that clear. *"And the great dragon was cast out, <u>that old serpent, called the Devil, and Satan</u>, which deceiveth the whole world: he was cast out into the earth, and his angels were cast out with him."* Verse 3 tells us that he had 7 heads which picture wisdom. He is no dummy. He is not omniscient but has much wisdom. God created him that way (Ezek. 28:12 & 17). He has 10 horns indicating universal power. He has millions of demons who jump at his command. He is the god of this world system (2 Cor. 4:4). He is the prince of the power of the air (Eph. 2:2). He is the prince of this world (Jn. 12:31). <u>We Christians are fighting against spiritual wickedness in high places (Eph. 6:12). At the time of his rebellion when he was kicked out of heaven, he drew a third part of the stars of heaven (Satan's angels).</u> Satan has been after the woman (Israel) ever since Gen. 3:15: *"And I will put enmity between thee and the woman, and between thy seed and her seed; it shall bruise thy head, and thou shalt bruise his heel."* This is also Jewish history. During this final 42-month period the *"Great Tribulation"* takes place. <u>From this point the last half of the tribulation starts.</u> God's people will need protection, so just as God took care of them for 40 years in the wilderness, He will care for them now during the last 3 ½ years of this Great Tribulation (Jer. 30:7). *Alas! for that day is great, so that none is like it: it is even the time of Jacob's trouble; but he shall be saved out of it,* (Dan. 12:1). Mt. 24:22, *And except those days should be shortened, there should no flesh be saved: but for the elect's sake those days shall be shortened.*

III. WAR IN HEAVEN VS. 7-9.

Where does this war take place? <u>It can't be in the 3rd Heaven where God sits on His throne.</u> Satan and his angels were cast out into the 1st and 2nd heavens (the aerial and stelar heavens) where he is called *"The prince of the power of the air."* <u>I am sure the devil will not like us being shot through his territory, the 1st and 2nd heavens at the rapture, but he'll have no power to stop us.</u> All this takes place during the last 3 ½ years of the Great Tribulation. <u>The devil is against us and especially Israel. But God is greater than the devil.</u> As I study and write these 7 sermons on the Revelation, I know he doesn't like it and I feel he is trying to stop me, but God is with me, and He is helping me. I am saying, "You old devil, get out of here! Your day is coming. Your destiny is sealed."

IV. THE VICTORIOUS CRY FROM HEAVEN – vs. 10-13

1. There is a cry of victory and praise to God because the devil was cast out of the first and second heavens to the earth. Now he knows his time is limited and <u>he has great wrath because he knows his time is short.</u> Rev. 12:12, *Therefore rejoice, ye heavens, and ye that dwell in them. Woe to the inhabiters of the earth and of the sea! for the devil is come down unto you, having great wrath, because he knoweth that he hath but a short time.* <u>The Greek for "wrath" is "boiling rage."</u> So, during this last half of The Tribulation, he will do all that he can to hurt Israel.

2. <u>The name "devil" means "slanderer" or, "false accuser" in the English Bible. Devil is translated from the word "diabolos" or "devil."</u>

3. <u>The only way to defeat the devil in that day will be by the blood of the Lamb (v.11).</u>

V. THE WINGS OF A GREAT EAGLE vs.14-17

1. <u>My favorite bird is the eagle.</u> In these verses God is protecting his people, Israel because of his great love. The Eagle's wings probably indicate an airlift or some

other miraculous speedy escape. Reminds me of Exo. 19:4,

"Ye have seen what I did unto the Egyptians, and how I bear you on eagles wings, and brought you unto myself."

VI. HOW GOD PROTECTS ISRAEL.

1. I think that verse 15 is literal. I believe that the devil is making an effort to destroy Israel by a flood. Yes, the devil has power, but it is limited by God. It reminds me of 1 Jn. 4:4. *Ye are of God, little children, and have overcome them: because greater is he that is in you, than he that is in the world.* I quote this many times.

2. The Bible tells us in Isaiah 59:19, *"when the enemy shall come in <u>like a flood</u>, the Spirit of the Lord shall lift up a standard against him."*

I always say, "If God be for us, who can be against us."

3. God causes the earth to help the woman, and the Dragon was wroth with the woman and does all he can to hurt her. <u>It could be that this is where the woman (Israel) flees to Petra for protection.</u>

CHAPTER 13

THE HEADED BEAST, WORLD GOVERNMENT, 42 MONTHS, LAMB/DRAGON, FALSE PROPHET.

We now come to chapter 13. I believe chapter 13 is full of signs and symbols that many theologians differ in what they think concerning the meaning.

I have had to sit back and read the chapter over and over again while asking the Lord to help me rightly divide the word of truth. I know you will agree with me that Revelation 12 was interesting. We saw how that the devil, all through the ages has made war with "the woman" who is Israel and how that God has protected Israel. We also read about the great Dragon (Anti-God) making war in the first and second heavens and how that Michael and his angels fought against him and that he was cast out of his so-called "kingdom" and cast to the earth. Then comes the cry to those on earth, *"Woe to the inhabitants of the earth and to the sea! for the devil is come down unto you, having great wrath, because he knoweth that he hath but a short time* (12:12). Then we see how that "the woman" (Israel) flees into the wilderness where the Lord cares for her 3 ½ years. So now we come to chapter 13. But don't jump the gun now and think that the seven bowls of judgment will be poured out on the earth right now. That doesn't take place until chapter 16:14-15. I find myself with my hands on the keyboard ready to type, but I have to push away from the desk, sit back, and attempt to take an overall view of what I am about to say. All I can do is to ask God for wisdom. Since chapter 13 has to do with two beasts, I'll have to divide this message up into two parts. The first is the antichrist and the second is the false prophet. The first beast is political, the second is religious. Both are energized by the power of Satan. Thus we have here an unholy Trinity; the devil, the antichrist and the false prophet.

I. THE FIRST BEAST – ANTI-CHRIST – vs. 1-10

1. In 13:1 we read *"and I stood upon the sand of the sea, and saw a beast rise up out of the sea..."* John is writing, but there is no need for John to stand on the sand and the sea. Actually, I think the verse should be translated as "and he stood upon the sand of the sea..." The original Greek personal pronoun is "it" but could be translated "he" referring to the Dragon (Satan). By standing on the sands of the sea, he is declaring that he is the supreme ruler of all peoples of the earth, but he is not supreme.

2. This first beast, the Antichrist rises out of the sea (the sea often represents Gentile nations). Rev. 17:8 tells us. *"The beast that thou sawest was, and is not; and shall ascend out of the bottomless pit and go into perdition: and they that dwell on the earth shall wonder, whose*

names are not written in the book of life from the foundation of the world, when they behold the beast that was, and is not, and yet is."

3. The 7 heads will be upon the antichrist because he will carry within himself and incorporated his last world Empire, the sum total of each past six governmental world kingdoms of past history. Here they are <u>Greece, Persia, Babylon, Assyria, Egypt and the Roman empire</u>. That's six. <u>The "beast" world Empire will be the 7th</u>. This 7th head (or kingdom), will include all the six world empires which have preceded this last world Empire.

4. This 7th head, or kingdom, according to Rev. 17:9 has an additional meaning. <u>It says that the 7 heads are 7 mountains.</u> These are literal hills or mountains, and it can be none other than ROME! Why Rome? Where on earth today do people look for a religion center? Of course, I do not consider Rome to be my religious center.

5. The seven heads therefore have a double meaning.

1. Political sovereignty.
2. The 7 mountains of Rome.

So, we are talking about the old Roman Empire being revived, but it will be worldwide in scope. <u>Even the Roman Empire in Jesus day was considered worldwide.</u>

6. The 10 horns - I believe the sea of verse one is the Mediterranean Sea and the nations in that general area will comprise of the 10 nations or kings. <u>The 10 horns of Revelation 13 are the same as the 10 toes in Daniel's image (Daniel 7:8) and speaks of a "little horn" (antichrist), and that he will come out of the 10 horns.</u> These 10 horns will come to power under antichrist at the middle of the tribulation. <u>I believe these 10 may be the</u>

world Federation of nations, or maybe the European common market composed of 10 nations. I am not sure, but I believe that already nine of them have been decided. One more, which I believe to be Greece, may be the 10th.

7. I spent more time on verse 1 on purpose because I want to know who this terrible beast is who will come up out of the sea.

8. Here in verse 2 we have a world dictator – the antichrist – ruling over the 10-nation federation which consists of the revival of the old Roman Empire. These nations are presently being formed in Europe today. Let me tell you something, the world is getting ready for the arrival of the antichrist. I believe that joining in any federation in Europe today is not advisable and is the wrong thing to do.

9. Verse 3 says, *"And I saw one of his heads as it were wounded to death; and his deadly wound was healed: and all the world wondered after the beast."* However, a resurrection takes place. I'm sure you know why. The antichrist is a counterfeit of everything concerning Christ. By performing this resurrection, the world is amazed and will follow his leadership.

10. Here is a synopsis of this beast and his activities:

(1) He appears on the scene in the "latter times" of Israel's history (Dan. 8:23).

(2) He will not appear until the Day of the Lord has begun (2 Thes. 2:2).

(3) His manifestation is being hindered by the Restrainer (2:6-7). God is in control and can stop the antichrist at His will.

(4) This appearance will be preceded by a departure (2

Thes. 2:3), which could have two meanings: a departure of the saints from the faith and/or the departure of the saints into glory at the rapture (2 Thes. 2:1).

(5) He may be a Gentile since he arises out of the sea (Rev. 13:1), and since the sea depicts the Gentile nations (17:15), he must be of Gentile origin.

(6) He rises from the Roman empire, since he is a ruler of the people who destroyed Jerusalem (Dan. 9:26).

(7) He is the head of the last form of Gentile world dominion, for he is like a leopard, a bear, and a lion (Rev. 13:1). As such he is a political leader. The 7 heads and 10 horns (Rev. 13:1; 17:12) are federated under his authority.

(8) His influence is world-wide, for he rules over all nations (Rev. 13:9). This influence comes through the alliance which he makes with other nations (Dan. 8:24; Rev. 17:1).

(9) He has eliminated 3 rulers in his rise to power (Dan. 7:8,24).

(10) His rise comes through his peace program (Dan. 8:25).

(11) He personally is marked by his intelligence and persuasiveness (Dan. 7:8,20; 8:23) so that his position over the nations is by their own consent (Rev. 17:13).

(12) He rules over the nations in his federation with absolute authority (Dan. 11:36). This authority is manifested through the change in law and customs (Dan. 7:15).

(13) The chief interest is in might and power (Dan. 11:38).

(14) As the head of the federated empire he makes a 7-

year covenant with Israel (Dan. 9:27), which is broken after 3 ½ years (Dan. 9:27).

(15) He introduces an idolatrous worship (Dan. 9:27) in which he sets himself up as God (Dan. 11:36,37; 2 Thes. 2:4; Rev. 13:5).

(16) He bears the characterization of a blasphemer because of his assumption of deity (Ezek. 28:2; Dan. 7:25; Rev. 13:1).

(17) He is energized by Satan (Ezek. 28:9-12; Rev. 13:4), and he receives his authority from him, and is controlled by the pride of the devil (Ezek. 28:2; Dan. 8:25).

(18) He is the head of Satan's lawless system (2 Thes. 2:3) and his claim to power and to deity is proven by signs wrought through satanic power (2 Thes. 2:11).

(19) He is received as God and as ruler because of the blindness of the people (2 Thes. 2:11).

(20) He becomes the great adversary of Israel (Dan. 7:21,25; 8:24; Rev. 13:7).

(21) There will come an alliance against him (Ezek. 28:7; Dan. 11:40,42) which will contest his authority.

(22) In the ensuing conflict he will gain control over Palestine and adjacent territory (Dan. 11:42) and will make his headquarters in Jerusalem (Dan. 11:45).

(23) At the time of his rise to power, he is elevated through the instrumentality of the harlot, the corrupt religious system, which consequently seeks to dominate him (Rev. 17:3).

(24) This system is destroyed by the ruler so that he may rule unhindered (Rev. 17:16,17).

(25) He becomes the special adversary of the Prince of

Princes (Dan. 8:25).

(26) While he continues in power for 7 years (Dan. 9:27), his satanic activity is confined to the last half of the Tribulation Period (Dan. 7:25; 9:27; 11:36; Rev. 15:5).

(27) His rule will be terminated by a direct judgment from God (Ezek. 28:6; Dan. 7:22,26; 8:25; 9:27; 11:45; Rev. 19:19,20). This judgment will take place as he is engaged in a military campaign in Palestine (Ezek. 28:8,9; Rev. 19:19) and he will be cast into the lake of fire (Rev. 19:20; Ezek. 28:10).

(28) This judgment will take place at the second advent of Christ (2 Thes. 2:8; Dan 7:22) and will constitute a manifestation of His Messianic authority (Rev. 11:15).

(29) The kingdom over which he ruled will pass to the authority of the Messiah and will become the kingdom of the saints (Dan. 7:27).

The rest of chapter 13 describes Satan's aggressive and fierce opposition to Christ and to those who follow him. In verses 4 to the rest of the chapter we read about how that the dragon and also the beast worshipped Satan and the Antichrist. The Antichrist was given power to speak great things and blasphemies against God. <u>Now that's dangerous. Yet people do that today.</u> <u>He had power to make war with the saints and he had power over all kindreds and tongues and nations.</u> <u>The whole world will worship him during that time and especially those whose names are not written in the book of the Lamb slain from the foundation of the world.</u> Then in verse nine we read, "If any man have an ear, let him hear." People today are not listening.

II. THE SECOND BEAST – THE FALSE PROPHET (ANTI-HOLY SPIRIT) -vs. 11-18.

Then in verse 11 another beast comes out of the earth having two horns like a lamb but he spake like a dragon. I believe that to be the false prophet which we might call the anti-holy spirit. Verse 11 says that he has two horns like a lamb. I believe the 2 horns signify power. There will be a religious power system on earth at this time. There will be the false one-world-church system that is set up during the first half of this period and the new Antichrist worshipping system enforced by this false prophet. I say, "Watch out for the NCC or WCC." I could mention Mt. 24:24 here. *"For there shall arise false Christ, and false prophets, and shall show great signs and wonders; insomuch that, if it were possible, they shall deceive the very elect."* He does great wonders so that he can make fire come down from heaven on the earth. He deceives people on the earth by means of miracles. He encourages people to make an image to the beast. (I have seen the great image of Buddha in Kamakura, Japan. It is huge. I've been inside the image and looked out the head. I saw people worshipping below). This image we are talking about here makes the Japan Buddha pale in comparison. He even had power to give life unto the image of the beast and that the beast image could speak. He caused everybody who would not worship the image to be killed. And this is where the mark of the beast shows up. This anti-Holy Spirit then causes everybody, rich and poor, free and bond, to receive a mark in their right hand or in their foreheads. Only those with the mark were able to buy or sell. And in verse 18 we are told that the number of the beast is 600 threescore and six or, 666. I believe Anti-Christ will know who has his mark and who does not. Come to think about it…look at your driver's license. I had to get a new mark on mine. They claim it's a new ID. Really? Some people can merely press their finger print on a document and it becomes legal. Listen, we are already programed to take the mark. DON'T BE DECEIVED!

CONCLUSION: Are you ready? (Isa. 55:6) *"Seek ye the Lord while he may be found, call ye upon him while he is near."*

REMEMBER THIS! WE WHO ARE SAVED WON'T BE THERE!

THE REVELATION OF JESUS CHRIST SERIES
FIFTH SUNDAY

CHAPTER 14 THE 144,000, 6 ANGELS, CHRIST REAPS THE HARVEST.
CHAPTER 15 7 VILES GIVEN TO 7 ANGELS, VICTORIOUS SAINTS, SONG OF MOSES.
CHAPTER 16 VIALS OF WRATH, FULL-JUDGMENT: SORES, SEAS, RIVERS, SUN, DARKNESS, ARMAGEDDON, EARTHQUAKES, HELL.

Now the scene changes from the mark of the beast to Jesus and 144,000 who follow the Lamb (Jesus Christ). The last chapter (13), was full of the beast, the anti-christ, the false prophet and dismal things. I didn't enjoy chapter 13, but chapter 14 gives encouragement. I am sure that you remember that chapter 13 was a rather alarming chapter. Here in chapter 14, the account of the closing of the tribulation, but don't think the Tribulation is over yet. It is merely mentioned, although it has not yet taken place at this point. I have an idea that John needed some kind of encouragement after having to write all about what happened in chapter 13. Chapter 13 was a horrible chapter telling of the beast that came out of the sea and the beast that came out of the land, the antichrist and the false prophet. Their deception, their horror, and their mark, the 666 are in chapter 13. But here now we have a contrast! Someone said, "the blackest storms often give place to the most beautiful sunsets." Shining through the dark clouds the ray of light appears. Chapter 13 with its horrors gives way to chapter 14. The wild and savage beast gives way to the gentle and loving Lamb. Those who confess and worship the beast who have received his mark gives way to the company of the Lamb's followers with his mark written on their foreheads. The worshiping of idols and trampling underfoot all that is holy gives way to the virgin purity which refuses to give in to the prevailing fornication and lifestyles promoted by the beast. The new order of things set up by the antichrist give way to "new song" of the redeemed. So I say, "Wow! Praise the Lord for chapter 14."

Chapter 14

I. THE 144.000 – vs. 1-5.

(**1**) These 144,000 are the same as those in chapter 7, God's people, the Jews, <u>whom He has sealed before the Great Tribulation (last half of the Tribulation); and whom he promised to protect against whatever their enemies would throw against them.</u>

(2) They have the name of the Lamb and the name of His Father written on their foreheads. Today the average Jew ridicules the belief of the scriptures, especially the New Testament.

(3) They were males who had never been married. The Bible makes it clear that the act of marriage is pure and holy. The Bible says that "the bed is undefiled." That means that these 144,000 Jews has to do with purity as far as their testimony is concerned.

(4) They are truthful as we see in *"in their mouth was found no guile* (5a). Today, where is truth? I heard a judge say, "Raise your right hand. Do you swear that what you are about to say is the truth?" What happened to "Please place your hand on the Bible. Do you swear that what you are about to say is the truth, the whole truth

and nothing but the truth, <u>so help me God?</u>"

II. THE EVERLASTING GOSPEL – 14:5-7.

(1) In verse 6, we see that God used an angel to preach His word. *"And I saw <u>another angel</u> fly in the midst of heaven, having the <u>everlasting gospel to preach</u> unto them that dwell on the earth, and to every nation, and kindred, and tongue, and people."* Verse 6 calls our attention to "another angel." <u>It might interest you to know that the Book of Revelation mentions "angel" 53 times, 203 times in the entire Bible. That means one quarter of the times an angel is mention, it is in the Revelation.</u> If we count the number of times <u>angel or angels</u> appear in the entire Bible, we see 297 times. Yes, God can and did use angels to preach. Luke 19:40 tells how He can use the stones to preach. In Numbers 22 the Lord opens the mouth of a donkey and causes him to speak. But today, he uses you and me.

(2) <u>What is the everlasting gospel?</u> 1 Cor. 15:1-4 answers that question.

1 Moreover, brethren, I declare unto you the gospel which I preached unto you, which also ye have received, and wherein ye stand; 2 By which also ye are saved, if ye keep in memory what I preached unto you, unless ye have believed in vain. 3 For I delivered unto you first of all that which I also received, how that Christ died for our sins according to the scriptures; 4 And that he was buried, and that he rose again the third day according to the scriptures. So, the gospel is the same we preach today. The Everlasting Gospel, with an Everlasting Message guaranteeing an Everlasting Salvation in an

Everlasting Home in heaven needs to be preached today.

III. THE FALL OF BABYLON – v.8.

(1) Who is Babylon? Chapters 17 & 18 have much to say about her and we will study that then, but for now just a few remarks.

(2) There are 2 Babylons in Revelation. <u>Both are called "Babylon the Great." Both are destined for destruction.</u> Here we are talking about religious Babylon. The other Babylon is the literal city of Babylon mentioned in Rev. 16. Antichrist will made use of this commercial center of the world. Isa. 13,14, etc. prove this. It will be destroyed at the end of the Tribulation Period. <u>We will study about Babylon later, but for now the picture before us is of a one-world church united to a one-world political system.</u> The present ecumenical effort attempting to unite all religions under the "Fatherhood of God and the brotherhood of man" is leading up to this end-time monster who makes all nations drink of the wine of her wrath.

IV. THE DOOM OF THE ANTICHRIST WORSHIPPERS AND THE BLESSEDNESS OF THE DEAD WHO DIE IN THE LORD – 9-13.

(1) These verses are self-explanatory. <u>What horror awaits those who worship the beast and his image and receive his mark, the 666!</u>

Rev. 14:9-11 *And the third angel followed them, saying with a loud voice, If any man worship the beast and his image, and receive his mark in his forehead, or in his hand,* 10 *The same shall drink of the wine of the wrath of God, which is poured out without mixture into the cup of his indignation; and he shall be tormented with fire and brimstone in the presence of the holy angels, and in the presence of the Lamb:* 11 *And the smoke of their torment ascendeth up for ever and ever: and they have no rest day nor night, who worship the beast and his image, and whosoever receiveth the mark of his name.*

Mockers need to know that there is coming a time when God calls it quits and exercises strong horrible judgment on unbelievers. So, I say, "make fun now; your day is coming!"

(2) But the believers who die in the Lord will be blessed.

Today we need patience to go through the trials of life. We have it easy compared to the saved who endure the miseries of life under the hellish rule of the Beast.

V. THE WHITE CLOUD, THE GOLDEN CROWN AND THE SHARP SICKLE, THE BATTLE OF ARMAGEDDON FORTOLD – 14:14-20

(1) The hour of judgment is come, and Babylon is on the brink of her fall and the damnation of every worshipper of the Beast and False Prophet.

(2) Here in 14:14 we see the Lord Jesus sitting on a white cloud with a crown upon His head. He has everything in control, so He sits on a cloud. Today we are watching for His coming at the rapture in the clouds.

(3) He has a sharp sickle in his hand indication He is about to reap. People cannot get away with their sins forever. The Bible says in Num. 32:23 *"Be sure your sin*

will find you out." I remember singing "Oh be careful little hands what you do; oh be careful little feet where you go, oh be careful little mouth what you say, for your Father up above looking down in love, do be careful little mouth what you say." That's not exactly correct, but it works for me.

(4) Armageddon Foretold and will happen – vs. 16-20. The conflict begins in the Valley of Jehoshaphat and centers in the Valley of Jezeel, which is on the plain of Esdraelong near the hill of Megiddo (16:16). Notice Joel 3:10-14. 10 *Beat your plowshares into swords, and your pruninghooks into spears: let the weak say, I am strong.* 11 *Assemble yourselves, and come, all ye heathen, and gather yourselves together round about: thither cause thy mighty ones to come down, O LORD.* 12 *Let the heathen be wakened, and come up to the valley of Jehoshaphat: for there will I sit to judge all the heathen round about.* 13 *Put ye in the sickle, for the harvest is ripe: come, get you down; for the press is full, their vats overflow; for their wickedness is great.* 14 *Multitudes, multitudes in the valley of decision: for the day of the LORD is near in the valley of decision.*

Eventually the battle encompasses the entire nation of Israel and is, of course, global in involvement as the armies of the world meet in the Middle East for the final holocaust of history – The Battle of Armageddon. In Zec.14:2 we read *"For I will gather all nations against Jerusalem to battle; and the city shall be taken, and the houses rifled, and the women ravished; and half of the city shall go forth into captivity, and the residue of the people shall not be cut off from the city."* The result is a

200 mile long area soaked with blood. <u>Did you know that Israel is 200 miles long? It will take 7 months to bury the dead. Right now, nations are lining up and getting ready.</u>

CHAPTER 15

<u>Chapter 15 is there to prepare us for chapter 16 which actually gets us into the horrible vials or bowls judgments.</u> Chapter 15 prepares us for what happens when the wrath of God is poured out on this earth using 7 vials or bowls. <u>I believe chapter 15 is a warning chapter. No way can man say there was no warning.</u> (If I saw someone coming after me with a gun; that would be warning enough, and I would take cover). A person who will not heed the warning is like someone who breaks the door to the roof of a 20 story building and jumps to his death.

6 There are 7 main judgments in the Bible.
1. The judgment of the believers at the cross.
2. The believers' self-judgment.
3. The judgment of the believer's works.
4. The judgment of the nations at the return of Christ.
5. The judgment of Israel at the return of Christ.
6. The judgment of angels.
7. The judgment of the wicked dead.
<u>NO ONE CAN CLAIM THEY WERE NOT WARNED.</u>

I would think that those living when those 7 angels in verse 1 showed up with those 7 last plagues with the wrath of God, that they would fall on their faces and repent. We will see that these last 7 plagues will be far more horrible than the seals and trumpet judgments during the first half of the Tribulation.

I. THE VICTORIOUS MARTYRS. 15:2-4.

In verse 2 we see those who had gotten the victory over the beast, the Antichrist. They are standing on a sea of glass mingled with fire. It could be that the sea of glass typifies the Word of God and the fire is indication of the fiery trials they endured at the hands of the Antichrist. They refused the mark and suffered martyrdom. They have the harps of God. They were those who refused the mark of the beast and heeded the preaching of the 2 witnesses and the 144,000 during the first half of the Tribulation. But now, remember Satan has been cast down from the 1st and 2nd heavens to the earth. He now knows his end is near, so he is doing all he can to fight against Almighty God. So, this is the last 3 ½ years of the Tribulation. They sing the song of Moses which is the celebration of Jehovah's victory over Israel's enemies, and the song of the Lamb which is the song of redemption. They are the ones who were slain because they would not give in to Satan. It reminds me that we too, need to take a stand against the devil and not give in to his temptations. It might seem hard now to take a stand for the Lord, but it will be far worse during this Great Tribulation. In 15:7, we are introduced to the 7 angels with golden vials with the 7 plagues ready to be poured out on the inhabitants of the earth.

Chapter 16

THIS CHAPTER OPENS WITH THE 7 BOWLS OF WRATH BEING POURED OUT ON THE EARTH.

If you think that the 7 seals and 7 trumpets were horrible, these 7 bowl judgments will be many times worse.

I need to once again make it clear that we Christians will not go through this terrible seven-year tribulation period. We will be with the Lord at the Judgment Seat of Christ. I remind you of this because of the most horrible time this world will ever go through. So, we Christians, can echo the words of the apostle Paul in Titus 2:13. *"Looking for that blessed hope, and the glorious appearing of the great God and our Savior Jesus Christ."*

I. GOD'S HOLINESS AND MAN'S REBELLION DEMAND HIS RIGHTEOUS JUDGMENTS UPON THE EARTH – 16:1.

1. Here we hear the very voice of God calling from the smoke-filled Temple with orders to the 7 angels to perform their duties. Why?

(1) Man slandered God and his holy laws by turning

from him to worship the Antichrist and his image, called by Matthew *"the abomination of desolation."*

(2) As a Holy God He cannot allow this sin to go unpunished. Notice these scriptures:

(Exo. 20:4-6): 4 *Thou shalt not make unto thee any graven image, or any likeness of anything that is in heaven above, or that is in the earth beneath, or that is in the water under the earth: 5 Thou shalt not bow down thyself to them, nor serve them: for I the LORD thy God am a jealous God, visiting the iniquity of the fathers upon the children unto the third and fourth generation of them that hate me;*

6 *And shewing mercy unto thousands of them that love me and keep my commandments.*

Also, Isa. 42:8: *"I am the LORD: that is my name: and my glory will I not give to another, neither my praise to graven images."*

NOW COMES THE MOST HORRIBLE PART OF THE TRIBULATION:

II. THE FIRST BOWL JUDGMENT -v.2.

16:2 *And the first went, and poured out his vial upon the earth; and there fell a noisome and grievous sore upon the men which had the mark of the beast, and upon them which worshipped his image.*

(1) Has this ever happened before? Look at Exo. 9:8-11. 8*"And the Lord said unto Moses and unto Aaron, take to you handfuls of ashes of the furnace, and let Moses sprinkle it toward the heaven in the sight of Pharaoh.*

9 *and it shall become small dust in all the land of*

Egypt, and shall be a boil breaking forth with blaines upon man, and upon beast, throughout all the land of Egypt. 10 And they sprinkled it up toward heaven; and it became a boil, breaking forth with blaines upon man, and upon beast. 11 Also the magicians could not stand before Moses because of the boils; for the boils was upon the magicians, and upon all the Egyptians." What a price to pay for sin!

III. THE SECOND BOWL JUDGMENT – v.3.

16:3 And the second angel poured out his vial upon the sea; and it became as the blood of a dead man: and <u>every living soul died in the sea.</u>

1. What a scene! The sea became as blood and everyone in the sea died. <u>Some might say, "NEVER HAPPEN."</u> If you were to read Exo. 7:17-21, you will see that this same thing happened when <u>God used Moses to perform this miracle in order to persuade Pharaoh to let the Jews leave Egypt.</u>

2. Can you visualize what this would be like? Every living person who was in the sea; maybe on a cruise ship, or our sailors on board our aircraft carriers and those swimming in the oceans would all die. Then to make it worse, the seas became *"<u>as the blood of a dead man."</u>* *"AS BLOOD"* <u>means it is about the same as blood.</u> The blood would wash up on our shores. The stink of dead men and blood will infiltrate the entire world.

BUT REMEMBER THIS…WE CHRISTIANS WILL NOT BE HERE WHEN THAT HAPPENS.

IV. THE THIRD BOWL JUDGMENT – 16:4-7

And the third angel poured out his vial upon the rivers and fountains of waters; <u>and they became blood</u>. 5 And I heard the angel of the waters say, Thou art righteous, O Lord, which art, and wast, and shalt be, because thou hast judged thus. 6 For they have shed the blood of saints and prophets, and thou hast given them blood to drink; for they are worthy. 7 And I heard another out of the altar say, even so, Lord God Almighty, true and righteous are thy judgments.

Now, <u>the plague comes into all the countries of the world</u>. All rivers became blood, literal blood, not just AS blood. The great Mississippi River, all the rivers in America and in the entire world became blood. Unimaginable! Then even an angel in heaven cries out, *"Even so, Lord God Almighty, true and righteous are thy judgments."*

1. Puny man does not have all the facts and is therefore incapable of judging God.

2. This may sound horrible, but I will say it anyway. Those who worship the beast and who have shed the blood of God's people who take the mark of the beast, God now gives them all the blood they want. Drink to your heart's content! You deserve what you get. They took blood, now they get blood.

V. THE FOURTH BOWL JUDGMENT – 16:8-9.

Now comes the fourth bowl judgment; the greatest scorching heatwave in history. <u>We've had a heatwave back in 1980 when it was over 100 degrees for days. Crops were parched. In the south, many died. But this</u>

bowl judgment will be far worse.

1.The earth becomes so drastically hot during this judgment that God must alleviate the suffering by shorting the days. Listen to Mt. 24:22, *And except those days should be shortened, there should no flesh be saved: but for the elect's sake those days shall be shortened.*

Despite this horrible scorching heat, they repented not and blasphemed the God of heaven. NOW REMEMBER THIS, WE WHO ARE SAVED WON'T BE THERE!

VI. THE FIFTH BOWL JUDGMENT – 16:10-11.

10 *And the fifth angel poured out his vial upon the seat of the beast; and his kingdom was full of darkness; and they gnawed their tongues for pain,* 11 *And blasphemed the God of heaven because of their pains and their sores, and repented not of their deeds.*

1. Whereas the fourth bowl judgment produced a brightness of the sun that man has never experienced before. Here the fifth bowl judgment produces a darkness that man has never before experience from one extreme to the other. From one extreme to the other, extreme brightness to extreme darkness. Has this ever happened before? Look again at Exodus 10:21-23. 21 *And the LORD said unto Moses, Stretch out thine hand toward heaven, that there may be darkness over the land of Egypt, even darkness which may be felt.* 22 *And Moses stretched forth his hand toward heaven; and there was a thick darkness in all the land of Egypt three days:* 23 *They saw not one another, neither rose any from his place for three days: but all the children of Israel had light in their dwellings.*

2. This period of time is described as *"The Day of The LORD."* Amos tells us in 5:15 *"Woe unto you that desire the day of the Lord! To what end is it for you? The day of the LORD is darkness, and not light."*

3. Let me read, Joel 2:1-2, 1 *Blow ye the trumpet in Zion, and sound an alarm in my holy mountain: let all the inhabitants of the land tremble: for <u>the day of the LORD cometh</u>, for it is nigh at hand; 2 A day of darkness and of gloominess, a day of clouds and of thick darkness, as the morning spread upon the mountains: a great people and a strong; there hath not been ever the like, neither shall be any more after it, even to the years of many generations.*

4. <u>Despite this horrible darkness and much pain, they repented not and blasphemed God.</u>

VII. THE SIXTH BOWL JUDGMENT AND THE BATTLE OF ARMAGEDDON – 16:12-16.

Verse 12 immediately calls our attention to the first thing that takes place that makes Armageddon able to take place. <u>The Euphrates River is dried up making a way for the kings of the east to cross over.</u> Here is more about the

Battle of Armageddon.

1. When will Armageddon be fought? Here's the events of the end time.

(1) The first resurrection takes place.

(2) The translation of the living saints; you and me.

(3) The marriage supper of the Lamb.

(4) The Tribulation Period divided into 2 parts.

(5) Armageddon at the close of the Tribulation.

(6) The second stage of His return.

(7) The conversion of the Jews, the chaining of Satan and the establishment of His throne.

Other verses for your study are Joel 2:5-11

2. Some Greek scholars say the Greek word here for "battle" actually could also be translated "campaign." Even in our day, some wars have been called "campaigns." For instance, the Korean War was called by Truman a "campaign" but for those who fought in Korea, it was an outright war! I believe Armageddon is an all-out war against God and his people. There are actually four confederations that line up against Israel. They are the northern Confederation led by the King of the North, the southern Confederation led by the King of the South, the Western Confederation led by the King of the West (the beast, the Antichrist), and the Oriental Confederation led by the kings of the east. But you might say that there is a 5th king who enters the "battle" and he is the one who decides the outcome. I am sure you know that he is none other than the King of kings and Lord of lords, the Son of God, Israel's Messiah, the world's Savior. One thing for sure, WE WON'T BE THERE!

3. THE PARTICIPANTS OF THIS GREAT BATTLE:

(1) THE KING OF THE NORTH. He is not mentioned here, but other scriptures show that this is Russia.

(2) In Ezek. 38, Gog is the prince of Rosh, Meschech and Tubal. Gog is the prince, Magog is his land. Meschech has reference to Moscow. Russia is the only nation with this description.

(3) In Ezek 38:15, the military alliance is said to come *"out of the north parts."* Russia's allies are said to include Ethiopia, but not the one in Africa by that name, but to the land to the north of Israel formerly known as Cush. Other allies of Russia are said to be Gomer (Germany). The old Bible name for Libya is "Phut." It is located south of Russia in the general area of Persia. The last nation mentioned is Togomah, which comprises the nations which we now know as central Asia. These nations have always been the arch-enemy of Israel and are Russia's friends.

(4) All these nations have always been anti-God and very materialistic. Years ago, no one was interested in the land area of Israel. A professor at Baptist Bible College (sorry, I do not remember his name) made this quote. "During the first decade after Israel became a nation there was discovered a storehouse of spoil valued at $1,270,000,000,000 which was estimated as the wealth of the entire world. Ocean water usually contains 6 pounds of salt to every 100 pounds of water. But in the Dead Sea there are 27 pounds of salt to every 100 pounds of water. The Dead Sea is rich in Potash.

(5) This battle does not take place before the rapture.

(6) The mighty armies of Rush, Meshech, and Tubal will be unable to cope with the disasters that they will face. The destruction from this war (battle) will be so complete that the dead bodies of the enemies will be left for food for all kinds of ravenous birds and wild beasts.

(7) Israel will not have to defend themselves. The Lord will come to their rescue.

4. THE KING OF THE SOUTH.

(1) In Dan. 11:40-45 we see the King of the South is mentioned. This king is the King of Egypt. The contention will be over the land of Israel and against the world ruler (Dan. 11:16). Do you remember the six-day war in June 1967 when Israel defeated Egypt. You would think they learned their lesson.

5. THE KINGS OF THE EAST.

(1) Some differ on who these are, but I <u>believe, as do many others that they are Orientals. Three-fourths of the earth's population are in India, China, Indo-China, Indonesia and the other oriental nations.</u>

(2) The Euphrates River has always been a boundary between East and West. With this dried up, the Kings of the East can march across.

(3<u>) Years ago the countries of China, Japan, Korea, etc. were considered poor, uneducated and backwards countries.</u> NOT ANYMORE, <u>China now has an army of 200,000,000 soldiers. Japan is one of the most advanced countries in the world.</u>

6. THE KING OF THE WEST.

The King of the West is the king of the revised Roman Empire, the Beast, the Antichrist. He is anti-everything we know about Christ.

7. <u>THE KING OF KINGS</u>

The return of the Savior to destroy the armies of the Antichrist in the Battle of Armageddon which we have already discussed.

VII. A FEW THOUGHTS ABOUT REV. 16:12-21.

1. The area surrounding the Euphrates is where Iran, Iraq, and Syria are now. It is also

the location of ancient Persia. It is also the area where the Garden of Eden was. Satan's first devastating blow at the Lord and His creation was there. <u>Ps. 2:2-4 tells us how God acts when all the nations of the world line up against him.</u>

2. *The kings of the earth set themselves, and the rulers take counsel together, against the LORD, and against his anointed, saying, 3 Let us break their bands asunder, and cast away their cords from us. 4 He that sitteth in the heavens shall laugh: the Lord shall have them in derision.* <u>Does this sound like God is scared? We are on the winning side.</u> I have to laugh too at the puny efforts of all who by their thoughts think they can change what has happened as well as what will happen. No wonder God sits in heaven and laughs at such nonsense.

3. THE FROGS – 16:13. Why frogs? Well, I won't elaborate on the frogs. Many differ of the meaning of these frogs. <u>My thought is that these frogs, representatives of the Satanic trinity and are ultra dirty.</u> I believe sin will get so obnoxious and aids will increase more and more as we get close to the end. How can sin get worse? <u>I think we are at the door of the Tribulation. But, don't worry; the rapture comes first. These 3 frogs are demonic spirits from the devil.</u>

4. 16:15 is a call to watch; that is, be prepared. I think the meaning of *"keepeth his garments"* has to do with being clothed spiritually and ready for His coming.

VIII. THE SEVENTH BOWL JUDGMENT –16:17 21

I will now summarize these last five verses in chapter 16. A voice is heard coming from the throne of God in heaven saying, *"it is done."* God himself is satisfied with what He has done. When Jesus was crucified on the cross, he made a similar statement. He said, *"it is finished."* You can be sure that our Almighty God always accomplishes what He does. Whenever God speaks, you can be sure things will happen. We find in verse 18 *"And there were voices, and thunders, and great lightnings; and there was a great earthquake, such as was not since men were upon the earth, so mighty an earthquake, and so great."* So powerful were the words of God, that the earthquake divided the city of Jerusalem into three parts and the cities in the nation's suffered utter destruction. Remember Babylon? Well verse 19 tells us that God sure remembered Babylon. We'll see what happens to Babylon in our next message.

In verse 20 we read that every island "fled away" and even the mountains fell flat. WOW! When I read that I had to hold my head in my hands and cry, "Oh, me! Why?

Well, I am a missionary to Japan. I've lived in Japan for 25 years. I have experienced the thunders, lightnings and earthquakes many times. I can tell you for a fact, that when an earthquake hits and your house moves, it's an eerie feeling. So, when I read in God's Word that every island fled away, I get to wondering, "what about Japan?" What about the thousands of people that I saw bowing before idols, and climbing the many steps up to the temple, and bowing before Buddha and other idols? I personally hope and pray that there is a great revival in Japan before the Tribulation takes place and millions come to Christ and get saved.

Then in verse 21 we find that great hail fell among men. The weight of every stone was about a talent the Bible tells us. That's about 90 to 135 pounds each. The insurance companies will be flooded with requests for help. <u>All this is indication of the utter destruction of every spiritual and religious institution that man has built up apart from God.</u> It's the absolute overthrow of civilization, as we know it. You would think that man would repent to God, but they do not repent, they only blaspheme the God of heaven. Next week we will discover what God does to Babylon that will be a remarkably interesting message. As I read of all this devastation I wish I could warn everyone to get saved now.

REMEMBER THIS! WE WHO ARE SAVED WON'T BE THERE!

THE REVELATION OF JESUS CHRIST SERIES
SIXTH SUNDAY

CHAPTER 17 MYSTERY BABYLON THE GREAT
CHAPTER 18 BABYLON IS FALLEN
CHAPTER 19 MARRIAGE SUPPER OF THE LAMB

CHAPTER 17

THIRD, The doom of the False Prophet.
FOURTH, The doom of the Kings.
FIFTH, The doom of Gog and Magog.
SIXTH, The doom of Satan.
SEVENTH, The doom of the unbelieving dead.
This division goes through chapter 20.

In chapters 21 and 22, we will study about 7 new things. Now we come to Babylon in chapters 17 and 18. Our next lesson will be the last, so I will tell you, don't miss it.

CHAPTER 17 CONTINUED
ANCIENT BABYLON

The ancient city of Babylon originated just after the flood, in the land of Assyria. The capital city was originally called BAB-EL, meaning "GATE OF GOD." Later, by God's decree, the name was changed to BABEL, meaning "CONFUSION." (Gen. 11:9). Nimrod was responsible for the beginning of this city. Nimrod actually means "rebel." Cush was the name of his father and he was a rebellious man. You've heard of The Tower of Babel. Nimrod was the instigator of that. He wanted to build a tower that would reach into heaven. However, God put a stop to that. God *"confounded their language"* so they could not complete the task. God can do anything. I believed God, in a way, gave me the Japanese Language, although I had to study. Is this the same Babylon? Look into chapter 17.

II. MYSTERY BABYLON.

<u>Babylon is the bride of the Antichrist as the Church is the bride of Christ.</u> She is called *"MYSTERY BABYLON THE MOTHER OF HARLOTS AND ABOMINATIONS OF THE EARTH"* (Rev. 17:5). In fact, verse 5 emphasizes that with all capital letters. What a title! She is also referred to as *"The great whore that sitteth upon many waters"* in verse one. The word *"whore"* in this verse means harlot or prostitute. I think this is interesting enough to throw it in here. I'm sure you remember Belshazzar, King of Babylon in Daniel's day. How he threw a party and desecrated the holy vessels which his father Nebuchadnezzar had taken from the temple of God in Jerusalem. They drank wine from those holy cups and praised the gods of silver and gold. It is a fact that almost all false religions in the world have their origin in ancient Babylon. This feast that Belshazzar had was not just to put on display of authority and power, but it had a religious significance. It was a religious ceremony or festival. Belshazzar was not the only king at that time, but he was also the head or priest of a repulsive religious cult. Then suddenly they saw a hand, writing on the wall and the king's knees smote one against the other in fear. That's what Rev.17, verse 2 refers to. Here we are

reading about <u>Mystery Babylon, the mother of all false religions</u>. Here in Rev. 17, <u>this could also be the "one-world church." That's why many churches have no doctrine.</u> There is more talk today about combining all denominations into a <u>one world church</u>. The <u>National Council of Churches</u> and the <u>World Council of Churches</u> may be one step before joining such a group. Here is a summary of some of the things about this woman.

1. <u>The woman</u> (Rev. 17:1,2,15,18). This false church will be domineering. Her influence will extend over nations governments, and the lives of men.

2. <u>Her character</u> (vs. 2). Fornication in a spiritual sense will be her great sin.

3. <u>Her power</u> (vs. 3). Here she controls the religious system.

4. <u>Her wealth</u> (vs. 4). This immense wealth may be a contributing factor to the <u>temporary alliance</u> between the beast-king and woman.

5. <u>Her name</u> (vs. 5). She is *"<u>mystery Babylon</u> the great, the mother of harlots, the abominations of the earth."*

6. <u>Her doom</u> (vs.16). <u>The beast-king, tired of the domination of the woman, turns upon her and eats her flesh and burns her with fire.</u>

7. <u>Not content with the destruction of the woman, the beast and his followers turn upon the Lamb</u> - *"The Lord of lords and King of kings."*

III. THE SUMNATION OF THIS CHAPTER

1. <u>The Bible tells us here in Rev. 17:7 that this woman has 7 heads and here in chapter 17, verse 9 we read,</u>

"And here is the mind that hath wisdom. The seven heads are seven mountains, on which the woman sitteth." <u>So, the headquarters for this world church can only be Rome</u> because Rome is the only city situated on 7 hills.

2. <u>Then we read about *7 kings: 5 are fallen, 1 is, and the other is not yet come; and when he comes, he will continue for a short time.*</u> Some consider (that is, think) the 5 that are fallen as: (1) Julius Caesar, (2) Tiberius, (3) Caligula, (4) Caudius, and (5) Nero. <u>Number 6, Domitian was, at the time John received this revelation, alive and on the throne. Number 7 is yet to come.</u> Remember chapter 13? He is the resurrected Antichrist.

3. <u>Then these with one mind give their power to the beast and make war with the Lamb, but the Lamb of God will overcome them (17:13-14).</u>

4. <u>The waters where the whore sits (vs.15) are peoples, multitudes, nations and tongues.</u>

5. <u>Verse 16 tells us that the antichrist eventually betrays his religious followers.</u> The world church shared the limelight with the beast during the first 3 ½ years of the Tribulation, but now the beast is tired of that and will hate the church, strip her of all possessions, (gold, precious stones, pearls) and destroy her by burning her remains in the ground. We see that in verse 16. *"And the ten horns which thou sawest upon the beast, these shall hate the whore, and shall make her desolate and naked, and shall eat her flesh, and burn her with fire."*

6. Verse 17 shows us that God is in control. <u>Despite the methods and manipulations of man, God's plan *will come to pass.*</u> Kings are but pawns in the game of life. *But God is the judge: he putteth down one, and setteth up*

another (Ps. 75:7); God moves the kings and rulers of this earth like a speaker moves the puppets that are dangling on strings. *The king's heart is in the hand of the LORD, as the rivers of water: he turneth it whithersoever he will* (Prov. 21:1). Wow! <u>We could say our president is decided by God.</u> God is in control. God was moving the strings of the puppets. In our elections God has a plan for this nation and this world and He is moving the rulers around to accomplish His will. I've said that many times. The end is near! When you begin to see these things come to pass, look up! <u>Luke 21:28</u> *And when these things <u>begin to come to pass</u>, then look up, and lift up your heads; for your redemption draweth nigh.* I firmly believe we are in the final days before Jesus comes for us in the rapture. All signs point to that now. The antichrist may already be in the world today. He will be revealed AFTER the rapture and we are gone, but NOT BEFORE! I firmly believe the way things are happening now, that the Rapture could happen at any moment. We are now in the last days.

CHAPTER 18

I. TWO DIFFERENT BABYLONS.

1. *"And after these things."* This shows that there should be no separation between chapter 17 and 18. The chapter divisions are not inspired.

2. *"I saw another angel come down from heaven"* (18:1). The angel in 17:1 is different than this one in 18:1.

3. The names of the two Babylons are different. The one in chapter 18 is *"Babylon, the great."* But the one in chapter 17 is *"Mystery Babylon, the great, the mother of harlots, and the abominations of the earth"* (17:5).

4. Babylon, the harlot of chapter 17 will be destroyed by the kings of the earth (17:16). The Babylon of chapter 18 will be destroyed by the judgments of God.

5. As for the destruction of Babylon of chapter 17, the kings of the earth will rejoice. The Babylon of chapter 18 will be destroyed by God, and the kings and merchants of the earth will weep for her (18:9-15).

6. The Babylon of chapter 17 will be destroyed in the middle of the tribulation so that the antichrist can set up his own religious system. That is, the one-world church

will be destroyed, and the antichrist will take over the religious system of the earth. The Babylon of chapter 18 will take place during the last half of the tribulation.

7. Therefore to sum up this point…chapter 17 describes the destruction of the religious system, whereas chapter 18 shows the destruction of Satan's seat, the commercial and governmental city of Babylon, and this comes at the end of the tribulation period. As I read chapter 17, I am once again, brought to the realization that this world is not getting better and better. 2 Tim. 3:13 *But evil men and seducers shall wax worse and worse, deceiving, and being deceived.*

II. BABYLON THE GREAT IS FALLEN – REV. 18:1-2

I am convinced that chapters 17 and 18 tell about two Babylons. Chapter 17 has to do with religious Babylon and chapter 18 deals with literal Babylon. I believe that the Babylon that is completely destroyed is religious Babylon. The literal city of Babylon will be rebuilt and then destroyed by the Lord at the end of the tribulation.

1. The angel who announces this is described as *"having great power and the earth was lightened with his glory"* (18:1). Surely this is Christ, himself. Look at John 8:12 where Jesus is called *"the light of the world."* But *then spake Jesus again unto them, saying, I am the light of the world: he that followeth me shall not walk in darkness, but shall have the light of life.*

2. There are many differences of opinion about this Babylon, but in this case, since Rome has never been thought to be a commercial city, but rather a religious city, I believe that this is literal Babylon rebuilt. But as I

already mentioned, Babylon will be permanently destroyed at the end of the tribulation. By the way, I will mention what I read about the rebuilding of Babylon on the internet. "In 1987, while on a site visit to the ruins of Nebuchadnezzar's palace, Saddam Hussein asked how his guides were so certain of the date of its construction. The curator showed Hussein some of the original bricks, stamped with the name Nebuchadnezzar II and the date that we now refer to as 605 B.C. Hussein, not to be outdone, had bricks laid at his palace wall that read: "In the reign of the victorious Saddam Hussein, president of the Republic, the guardian of the great Iraq and the renovator of its renaissance and the builder of its great civilization, and the rebuilding of the great city of Babylon was done in 1987." (Copied from an article entitled, "Babylon today, rebuilding the ancient city.") It is interesting to recall when the US military invaded the headquarters of Dictator Saddam Hussein in Iraq on Dec. 13, 2003 and captured him. On Dec. 30, 2006, he was finally hanged. Who would have thought that we, living today, would see that on our television sets? We are living in the last days. Jesus is coming soon. You can be sure Jesus will come and I'm looking for Him to come soon.

III. BABYLON TO BE REBUILT.

1. Isaiah 13 & 14 and Jer. 50 & 51 describe <u>the destruction of Babylon as being at the time of *"the day of the Lord"* which can only refer to the Tribulation period.</u>

2. Look at Jer. 51:26, *"and they shall not take of thee a stone for a corner, nor a stone for foundations, but thou*

shalt be desolate forever, saith the Lord." That is talking about the literal city of Babylon. Right now, at least six nearby cities have used the ruins of Babylon in the building of their city, including Bagdad, 50 miles north of Babylon. By doing so, they found great treasure and materials of the once beautiful buildings. So, this shows that the city of Babylon must be rebuilt. Then it is finally destroyed by the Lord in Revelation 18. No part of it will be used to build any of the city. That's when it will never be rebuilt again. In 18:4-5, God commands His people to come out of Babylon. Reminds me that we are commanded to come out of the world and be separate. False doctrines are already being taught today. So even more so, we need to be separate and to take a stand on "thus saith the Lord."

    3. The prophecies of Jeremiah back up this fact. Isaiah 13:19-20 says, "19 And *Babylon, the glory of kingdoms, the beauty of the Chaldees' excellency, shall be as when God overthrew Sodom and Gomorrah.* 20 *It shall never be inhabited, neither shall it be dwelt in from generation to generation: neither shall the Arabian pitch tent there; neither shall the shepherds make their fold there."* Ancient Babylon was never destroyed like that, so it will be rebuilt and then destroyed by God.

    4. Babylon today. The Iraqi government is building homes and moving its workers to bring old Babylon back to life. The ancient city of Babylon is being resurrected. Who does God use to order Babylon to be rebuilt? This is interesting, I got it from the internet. Babylon's remains, mounds of mud-brick buildings spread over about 30 square kilometers, are in present-day Iraq, south of

Baghdad. Starting in 1983, <u>Saddam Hussein,</u> imagining himself as heir to Nebuchadnezzar, ordered the rebuilding of Babylon.

5. <u>The one-world government, the one-world religion, the one-world banking system that makes possible the commerce of the world are already gathering momentum. It is just a matter of time before they decide to locate in one place; that place is Babylon. I believe we are seeing the foundation of the city of Babylon being resurrected.</u> Once again, we see the Bible is true. The writers of the Bible were inspired by God as they wrote His words.

IV. THE LITERAL DESTRUCTION OF BABYLON – 18:16-24.

1. Once rebuilt, this great city will serve as the seat of Satan.

2. <u>Babylon will be one of the most short-lived capitals of the world.</u> (Rev. 18:17-19) 17 *"For in one hour so great riches is come to nought. And every shipmaster, and all the company in ships, and sailors, and as many as trade by sea, stood afar off,* 18 *And cried when they saw the smoke of her burning, saying, What city is like unto this great city!* 19 *And they cast dust on their heads, and cried, weeping and wailing, saying, Alas, alas, that great city, wherein were made rich all that had ships in the sea by reason of her costliness! for in one hour is she made desolate."* <u>The merchants and sailors will cry over her, but God's people will rejoice over her (18:20).</u> We have already seen this by <u>earthquakes, thunder, lightning, plagues, death, mourning and famine</u>. Verse 16 says, *"she shall be utterly burned with fire."*

3. Verse 22 seems to indicate that Babylon will be the musical city of the world, but not for long. She will set the pace for music. If you think that most of the rock music is bad now, wait till Babylon music makes its debut, but we won't be here then.

4. Let me call your attention to an important thought. This is important. Notice Chapter 18 where we are studying now, vs. 4-5. *4 And I heard another voice from heaven, saying, Come out of her, my people, that ye be not partakers of her sins, and that ye receive not of her plagues. 5 For her sins have reached unto heaven, and God hath remembered her iniquities.* God is always merciful. These tribulation saints are warned not to partake of the sins of Babylon and to come out of her. This reminds me of 2 Co. 6:17 *Wherefore come out from among them, and be ye separate, saith the Lord, and touch not the unclean thing; and I will receive you.* <u>To leave the worldly things behind and be separate takes strong commitment.</u>

CHAPTER 19

THE WRATH ON EARTH AND THE REJOICING IN HEAVEN

I want to condense this chapter but since it is full of very important events, I must go into some details to help you understand. As I mentioned in chapter 18, the city of Babylon is destroyed, but then rebuilt and becomes the world's center of trade, commerce, wealth, and even becomes knows as the music center of the world. But remember this... (Gal. 6:7) *"Be not deceived; God is not mocked: for whatsoever a man soweth, that shall he reap."* God sits in heaven and laughs at man's opposition to him. (Ps. 2:4). *"He that sitteth in the heavens shall laugh: the LORD shall have them in derision."* God is in control. He has always been in control. He is in control now. Always put your trust in the Lord. I've heard it said, "I would rather fail now in a cause that is ultimately going to succeed, than to succeed now in a cause that is ultimately going to fail."

I. TO WHOM THE PRAISE IS GIVEN – 19:1

And after these things I heard a great voice of much

people in heaven, saying, Alleluia; Salvation, and glory, and honour, and power, unto the Lord our God:

1. *"Unto the <u>Lord our God</u>."* Is He your Lord? He is your God alright, but to make him Lord, you must make Him so.

2. <u>Three reasons for this phrase:</u>

(1) *"For true and righteous are His judgments."* In chapter 15:3, the harpers on the sea of glass sing, *"Righteous and true are thy ways."* In chapter 16:7, the alter says, *"True and righteous are thy Judgments."* <u>This means that all the seal judgments, trumpet judgments, vial judgments and all other judgments that have ever taken place on this earth to individuals, families, cities, countries are</u> *"true and righteous."*

(2) Look at verse 2. *"For true and righteous are his judgments: <u>for he hath judged the great whore, which did corrupt the earth with her fornication,</u> and hath avenged the blood of his servants at her hand."*

(3) Now the third reason for this phrase: *"And hast avenged the blood of His servants at her hand."*

II. THE FOUR ALLELUIAS AND THE MARRIAGE SUPPER OF THE LAMB – 19:1-10

1. The first *"Alleluia"* is praise to the Lord. And He is deserving of our praise.

2. The second *"Alleluia"* is their joy because God has judged the great whore that corrupted the earth. Our enemy, Satan, has done all he can to defeat Christ, <u>but he is judged, and all heaven rejoices.</u>

3. The third *"Alleluia"* is when the *"Four and twenty elders and the four beasts"* fall down and worship God.

I think that these "Alleluias" are a way to express their excitement that God has said "That's it, it's my turn now." Pro. 29:1 *He, that being often reproved hardeneth his neck, shall suddenly be destroyed, and that without remedy.*

4. The fourth *"Alleluia"* comes from *"a great multitude"* praising God *"as the voice of many thunderings."* They were rejoicing because *"the marriage of the Lamb is come and His wife hath made herself ready"* (19:6-10). This brings us to "the marriage supper of the Lamb" (19:9). That will not be compared with Cracker Barrel, Red Lobster, Golden Corral, or Braum's Ice Cream! (I just thought I'd throw that in, in case you were wondering). It will be "out of this world!"

III. MORE ABOUT THE WEDDING AND THE MARRIAGE SUPPER – 19:7-10

1. The Bridegroom. There is no controversy as to who this is. The Bridegroom is Jesus Christ.

2. The Bride. The identity of *"The Lamb's wife"* has been debated often. I will just mention briefly that some think the bride of Christ is Israel. Here are the verses that show otherwise: Hosea 4:6, Hosea 4:17, Hosea 5:3-6. Without hesitation, I say The bride of Christ is the Church.

3. So,The Bride is without doubt, the Church. 2 Cor. 11:2 tells us, *"For I am jealous over you with godly jealousy: for I have espoused you to one husband, that I may present you as a chaste virgin to Christ."* Another scripture is Eph. 5:32: *"This is a great mystery: but I speak concerning Christ and the Church."* Paul is

pointing out in this verse that the Lamb's wife can only be the Church.

4. By the end of the Tribulation Period, the Judgment Seat of Christ will have already taken place in heaven. Then Eph. 5:27 will be true: *"That He might present it to himself a glorious church, not having spot, or wrinkle, or any such thing; but that it should be holy and without blemish."* It can only be *"holy and without blemish"* after the judgment of the believers.

IV. THE MARRIAGE SUPPER.

1. You remember that Christ attended a marriage supper in Cana as recorded in John 2:1-12. It was the custom in those days for the bridegroom to have this feast at his home. It was an expensive undertaking. Here in America, we think the marriage supper is expensive, but we must take a back seat to Japan. In Japan, every guest receives a gift under his chair. The feast can cost thousands of dollars and all the presents can cost thousands of dollars. But this Marriage Supper in heaven and the reception will be unimaginable.

2. Will there be a honeymoon? We might say that The Thousand Year Millennial Reign of Christ will be the honeymoon. What do you think?

V. THE BATTLE OF ARMAGEDDON – 19:11-19

1. Now here comes a white horse with a rider called *"The Faithful and True"* (19:11). This can be none other than Jesus Christ. He doesn't come on a weak donkey as He did when he entered Jerusalem (Mk. 11:7-9). Here He comes riding a white stallion.

2. Notice His description (19:12-16). I would do injustice to this description if I didn't just read it to you.

12 His eyes were as a flame of fire, and on his head were many crowns; and he had a name written, that no man knew, but he himself. 13 And he was clothed with a vesture dipped in blood: and his name is called The Word of God. 14 And the armies which were in heaven followed him upon white horses, clothed in fine linen, white and clean. 15 And out of his mouth goeth a sharp sword, that with it he should smite the nations: and he shall rule them with a rod of iron: and he treadeth the winepress of the fierceness and wrath of Almighty God. 16 And he hath on his vesture and on his thigh a name written, KING OF KINGS, AND LORD OF LORDS.

VI. THE SUPPER OF THE GREAT GOD – 19:17-19)

1. This "supper" is far different than *"The marriage supper of the Lamb." An angel commands the fouls that fly in the midst of heaven, that they would eat the flesh of captains, horses and they that ride on them, and the flesh of all men both small and great.* In verse 19, we read, *And I saw the beast, and the kings of the earth, and their armies, gathered together to make war against him that sat on the horse, and against his army.*

VII. THE DOOM OF THE BEAST AND THE FALSE PROPHET – VS. 20

1. The end of the battle with victory for Christ and the armies of heaven is described in verse 20. The beast of Rev. 13:1-10 is taken and with him the false prophet, the

second beast of Rev. 13:11-16. The false prophet is identified as the one who wrought miracles and deceived them that received the mark of the image (13:12-15). The doom of the beast and the false prophet culminates in their being cast alive into the lake of fire burning with brimstone. The lake of fire is the final place for the wicked beast and false prophet. The beast and false prophet, the civil and religious leaders of the last league of nations, will be Satan inspired and Satan led them to their final doom.

CONCERNING THE MILLENNIAL REIGN OF CHRIST, <u>REMEMBER THIS! WE WHO ARE SAVED WILL BE THERE!
BUT WE WON'T BE THERE DURING THE BATTLE OF ARAMAGEDDON OR
THE DOOM OF THE BEAST AND THE FALSE PROPHET.</u>

THE REVELATION OF JESUS CHRIST SERIES
SEVENTH SUNDAY

CHAPTER 20 MILLENNIUM, SATAN BOUND 1000 YEARS, GOG & MAGOG, LAKE OF FIRE, THE GREAT WHITE THRONE JUDGMENT
CHAPTER 21 NEW HEAVEN & NEW EARTH
CHAPTER 22 NEW JERUSALEM, ETERNITY WITH CHRIST.

ANOTHER WAY OF EXPLAINING THESE THREE CHAPTERS IS THAT CHAPTERS 20, 21, AND 22 TELL US ABOUT THE END OF EVIL AND THE BEGINNING 0F ETERNAL JOY AND BLESSINGS IN THE NEW HEAVEN AND THE NEW EARTH.

CHAPTER 20

INTRODUCTION

Now we come to the final week, lesson 7, the conclusion to the Book of The Revelation.

I. SATAN CAST INTO THE BOTTOMLESS PIT vs. 1-3

1. <u>Satan bound for a thousand years. 20:1-3. God sends one angel to grab the dragon, that old serpent, which is the Devil and Satan, and bound him a thousand years (Rev. 20:1-2). God only needed one angel to do that.</u>

1 *And I saw <u>an angel</u> come down from heaven, having the key of the bottomless pit and a great chain in his hand. 2 And <u>he laid hold on the dragon, that old serpent, which is the Devil and Satan, and bound him a thousand years.</u>* Then verse 3 says, *"And cast him into the bottomless pit, and shut him up, and set a seal upon him, that he should deceive the nations no more, until the thousand years should be fulfilled: and after that he must be loosed a little season."*

(I'd like to help kick him in. He has attacked me all through my life.) But I must say, he has not stopped me from preaching His word. God shows his great power by sending just <u>one angel</u> to grab that dragon, that old serpent, which is the devil and Satan by his throat (that's my take on this) and bound him for 1000 years and cast him into the bottomless pit. That is the power of God. Zec. 4:6 *"... Not by might, nor by power, but by my spirit, saith the LORD of host."*

II. SATAN'S THOUSAND-YEAR- INCARCERATION IN PRISON 20:1-3

1. <u>The order of events described in Rev. 20</u>. I'll read this again because I like hearing about what happens to Satan.

(1) We see in 20:1-3 that Satan is bound for a thousand years. 1 *And I saw an angel come down from heaven, having the key of the bottomless pit and a great chain in his hand.*

2. *And he laid hold on the dragon, that old serpent, which is the Devil, and Satan, and bound him a thousand years,* 3 *And cast him into the bottomless pit, and shut him up, and set a seal upon him, that he should deceive the nations no more, till the thousand years should be fulfilled: and after that he must be loosed a little season.* Why must he be bound? Perhaps to prove the absolute justice of God in casting the wicked devil into the bottomless pit for a thousand years, but then after the Thousand-Year Millennial Reign of Christ, <u>he will be cast into the Lake of Fire</u> to suffer forever (vs. 10).

(2) For a thousand years (The Millennial reign of Christ) the devil will be bound, and therefore <u>during that time men will be free from his wicked influence. Finally, righteousness will reign when the King of kings and Lord</u>

of lords is in charge.

III. THE THOUSAND-YEAR MILLENNIAL REIGN OF CHRIST ON EARTH – 20:4-6

(1) During those 1000 years, Christ will reign in person on the earth.

(2) During that 1000 years the population of earth will increase. Countless children will be born during that time. All these children will have to be born again just as we do today. If they do not get saved, they will join with Satan when he is released.

(3) Everyone will worship King Jesus Christ, even those who are not saved.

(4) The atheist will bow before the King of kings.

Rom. 14:11, *For it is written, As I live, saith the Lord, every knee shall bow to me, and every tongue shall confess to God.* All Christ-rejectors will bow. The Pharaohs will bow. All enemies of Christ will bow. Those who have tried to destroy the church will bow. Those who cried, "Crucify him, crucify him" will bow. Also, sorry to say, but all those who you and I have witnessed to and have rejected Jesus will bow. They can cry all they want but, *"Oh, what a weeping and wailing, As the lost were told of their fate; They cried for the rocks and the mountains, They prayed, but their prayer was too late."* If you are concerned for your family and friends who are not saved, you better do all you can to get them saved now. Tomorrow may be too late.

(5) Verse 6 tells us that we who are raised in the first resurrection will be blessed and will be priests of God and of Christ and shall reign with Him during this

thousand years. So now we can sing.

"What a day that will be, When my Jesus I shall see, And I look upon his face, The one who saved me by his grace, When he takes me by the hand, And leads me through the Promised Land, What a day, glorious day that will be!" That's right. We who have been saved now and have been faithful to him, will help reign with him. Wow! What a day that will be!

(4) Today it is a common thing to hear of murder, drunks killing people, abortion, drugs, etc. During these thousand years when the devil is gone, those things will be rare, <u>but there will be some who will rebel.</u>

(5) Isaiah 11 tells us more about these 1000 years.

Isa.11:<u>6-7</u> 6 *The wolf also shall dwell with the lamb, and the leopard shall lie down with the kid; and the calf and the young lion and the fatling together; and a little child shall lead them. 7 And the cow and the bear shall feed; their young ones shall lie down together: and the lion shall eat straw like the ox.* WHAT A TIME!

(6) <u>However, sad to say, at the end of that 1000 years there will be a great multitude of men who have given only lip service to the King, whose hearts had never been changed and, who as a result are ready to follow Satan the moment he is released.</u>

IV. NOW COMES THE FINAL BATTLE 20:7-10.

1. When the 1000 Year Millennial Reign of Christ is over, then Satan will be released out of prison and will go about to deceive the nations. He will succeed in getting the nations together to fight against God (20:8). That's when the Gog and Magog war will take place.

2. <u>The number of the armies are "as the sand of the sea."</u>

3. Verses 9 and 10 indicate that this war will be worldwide. <u>It is said that the armies will "compass the saints and the beloved city", which must be Jerusalem.</u>

4. But despite the great number against the "beloved city," God will send fire out of heaven which devours them. Many times, the victories we experience now are not because of our efforts, <u>but it's all because God fighting for us</u>. If God be for us, who can be against us?

5. I sure like Rev. 20:10 – *"And the devil that deceived them was cast into the lake of fire and brimstone, where the beast and the false prophet are, <u>and shall be tormented day and night for ever and ever</u>."* Hallelujah!

V. THE GREAT WHITE THRONE JUDGMENT - 20:11-15

1. This is a passage that some <u>preachers don't want to mention and most people don't want to hear.</u>

2. Every man, woman who has rejected Christ will be there. From wicked Cain to the last one who rebelled with Satan at the end of the Millennium will be there. <u>It doesn't matter how an unsaved person's body is buried, or if the ashes are thrown into the deepest sea, or eaten by animals; they will be there to face judgment.</u> Num. 32:23, *But if ye will not do so, behold, ye have sinned the against LORD: and be sure your sin will find you out.* God is a righteous and loving God. Can you even imagine any unsaved sinner in heaven? 2 Pet. 3:9, *The Lord is not slack concerning his promise, as some men count slackness; but is longsuffering to us-ward, not*

willing that any should perish, but that all should come to repentance.

3. The unsaved bodies are in the graves, they are dead. Their souls are in hades (hell) and they are conscious. Their souls and bodies come together to stand judgment and to receive their final destiny. I'm glad I'm saved!

4. The books are opened and the book of life. Why is the *"Book of Life"* brought out? I believe to show them that not only are they judged by their evil deeds, but also to show them that their names are not written in the Book of Life. Praise the Lord, my name is in the Book of Life, and God doesn't have any erasers.

5. God's word seems to indicate that they will be assigned a degree of punishment based on many factors. How many opportunities each has had to accept Christ, and the degree and amount of sin they committed.

6. What about the heathen who are not saved? When they ask that question, they should first ask themselves, "Am I saved?" Why worry about the heathen? What ever torment the heathen endure, you who live in America and have heard the Gospel will be 10,000 time worse than their eternity if you continue to reject Jesus.

7. I urge you who are not saved, to get saved immediately. You have no idea when the rapture happens, and you are left behind. I advise you – Don't put off that decision, don't take a chance. Many times the Word of God tells us that today is the day to get saved. Why put it off when the door is open now?

CHAPTER 21

I. THE NEW HEAVEN AND THE NEW EARTH – 21.

1. Now we come to perhaps the most beautiful subject in the entire Bible. THE NEW JERUSALEM. I will read what I consider among the most comforting verses in the Bible. Rev 21:1-2 *1 And I saw a new heaven and a new earth: for the first heaven and the first earth were passed away; and there was no more sea. 2 And I John saw the holy city, new Jerusalem, coming down from God out of heaven, prepared as a bride adorned for her husband.*
I am sure you feel like I do. We are tired of this old earth with its nitty-gritty days filled with disappointments, health problems, hospital stays, discouragements, aches and pains, Covid-19 virus, and computer problems. In verses 9-10, we read that John was carried to a high mountain where he was privileged to see the holy city, the new Jerusalem descend out of heaven. He had the one and only first-class seat. Wow! What a scene. Not just any mountain, but a high mountain. God wanted him to see the New Jerusalem slowly descend from heaven. Wow! 21:9-1 *19 And there came unto me one of the seven angels which had the*

seven vials full of the seven last plagues, and talked with me, saying, Come hither, I will shew thee the bride, the Lamb's wife. 10 *And he carried me away in the spirit to a great and high mountain, and shewed me that great city, the holy Jerusalem, descending out of heaven from God,* 11 *Having the glory of God: and her light was like unto a stone most precious, even like a jasper stone, clear as crystal.* What a scene!

II. THE NEW JERUSALEM REV. 21:10-27

Oh, what a wonderful, magnificent, marvelous, glorious view we have here in chapter 21. When I finished the horrible events of the Tribulation Period and opened my Bible to chapter 21, and read those words, *"And I John saw the holy city, New Jerusalem coming down from God out of heaven, prepared as a bride adorned for her husband,"* I had to shout, Hallelujah." Sugoooi! (That's Japanese for "Wow!")

I have seen a lot during my 93 years. I've been to the top of the Empire State Building, walked through the hall of the capital building in Washington D.C., visited the Grand Canyon, went up the highest TV tower in the world at that time in Tokyo...but the view that John saw takes the cake. And just imagine, we will walk the golden streets in that great city, the New Jerusalem.

2. Let me tell you about that new Jerusalem.

(1) They'll be no more sea speaks of separation (v.1). Our soldiers won't have to go off to war and be separated from families. Our missionaries won't have to leave father and mother, to go to some mission field to spend a lifetime. There will be no more separation. In fact, there

won't be any need for missionaries.

(2) God himself shall dwell with people (v. 3).

(3) *No more tears, no more death, neither sorrow, nor crying, neither shall there be any more pain* (praise the Lord!), *for the former things are passed away* (v. 4). How many of you are looking forward to that wonderful day when we shall see Jesus and all the former things will be gone forever?

(4) Everything will be made new (v. 5). You will have a new home in glory that Jesus is preparing for us. It will be fully equipped. You will lack nothing. And I am sure it will be free. There will be room enough for the saved of all ages of time.

(5) A great and high wall will have 12 gates with the names of the 12 tribes of Israel written on them.

(6) The wall of the city will have 12 foundations with the names of the 12 apostles (v. 14).

(7) The city will be 1,500 miles high; the length and breath will be the same. What a massive city (v.16)!

(8) The wall will be of jasper and the city of pure gold, like unto clear glass (v. 18).

(9) The 12 foundations of the wall will each be garnished with precious stones. There will be jasper, sapphire, chalcedony, emerald, sardonyx, sardius, chrysolite, beryl, topaz, chrysoprase's, jacinth and amethyst. Twelve in all (vs. 19-20). A Jeweler I know in Mt. Vernon, Missouri said that he has never seen some of those jewels.

(10) The wall will have 12 gates which are the names of he 12 tribes of Israel and each gate was made of 1 big pearl (v. 21). I have never seen a Pearl bigger than me,

but God can make one big enough to be a door, and he doesn't need an oyster to do it, although he could just as easily make an oyster that big if he wanted. The Bible tells us that nothing is impossible with God.

(11) The streets of the city will be pure gold, like transparent glass (v. 21).

(12) There will be no temple because the Lord God Almighty and the Lamb are the temple (v. 22).

(13) The city doesn't need the sun, neither the moon, to shine in it: for the glory of God will lighten it, and the Lamb is the light there of (v. 23).

(14) The gates will not be shut at all by day: and there will be no night there (v. 25).

(15) And praise the Lord, *"there shall in no wise enter into it any thing that defileth, neither whatsoever worketh abomination, or maketh a lie: but they which are written in the Lamb's book of life"* (v. 27).

CHAPTER 22

We now come to this last chapter in the Bible and the last lesson of the Revelation. This closing chapter takes us to the end of our "Sightseeing Tour Through the Book of the Revelation" which I also like to call this study. Our wonderful future is described as we see The New Jerusalem and reaffirms the fact that only those who possess the righteousness of Christ by being born again are granted admittance and residence. I will take you through this chapter verse by verse.

VERSE 1-2 There will be a pure river of water of life flowing from the throne of God and the Lamb. I imagine it will be a beautiful sight; more beautiful than we now see here on earth. The water from that river will never stop flowing. (I have a glass of water by my desk that informs me when I need a drink. I'm not kidding.) But that water can't compare with that *"clear as crystal"* water from the throne of God. It will even taste better than coffee. Will we eat in heaven? Did not Jesus eat after he rose from the grave? He had a glorified body, and he ate. In Luke 24:41-43 Jesus asked the disciples if they had any meat? "They gave him a piece of broiled fish and a honeycomb and he ate it." The Bible says we will be like him (1 Jn. 3:2). <u>Verse 2 also says that on each side of the River of Life there will be a Tree of Life yielding 12 fruits. Wow!</u> On one tree, 12 different fruits! There would be no need to mention that there are 12 fruits if they were not edible. Our Bible says this fruit will be for the healing of the nations, "healing" could be translated "health." There won't be any need for healing! Adam and Eve were forbidden to eat from the *"tree of knowledge of good and evil"* (Gen. 2:17), and He placed an angel to keep them from eating the fruit from the *"Tree of Life."* But, praise God, no angel will prevent us from drinking from the clear as crystal River of Life and eating from the Tree of Life.

    <u>VERSE 3</u> The "curse" which originated in the Garden of Eden will be gone forever. *"There shall be no more curse."* All evil will be gone! You won't need any weapons for protection. You won't need to lock your door at night, if there are doors, and we know there will be no nights.

    <u>VERSE 4</u> *"They shall see his face."* We will see Jesus face to face. Wow! <u>I'm looking forward to seeing Jesus.</u> He's the first person I want to see when I get there. I'm sure you do too. When He looks at us, He will see His name inscribed upon our forefaces.

    "Face to face I shall behold him, the starry sky; face to face in all his glory, I shall see him by and by!"

    <u>VERSE 5</u> The light of our Savior will shine on us. <u>There will be no need of any artificial light.</u> Even the sun that has warmed the earth will not be needed. The love of God will warm us and will shine upon us forever. There will be no night there. If there is no night there, will we

need to sleep? I sure get tired now, but we won't get tired in heaven.

VERSE 6 Here John is allowed to see this vision to show that the vision is absolutely true because the "Lord God" cannot lie. He also mentions that these things will speedily come to pass. Nothing can stop what God will do. I believe it is not correct to say, "God said it, I believe it, that settles it." I believe that "God said it, that settles it, whether I believe it or not" is more correct.

VERSE 7 Just as in verse 6, the Lord told John that these things in the Revelation would happen speedily, so He also informs him that He will come speedily. *"Behold, I come quickly"* (speedily). The term "quickly" does not refer to days, months or years. Rather, it speaks of a series of events happening in rapid succession once they begin. In other words, when these things begin to come to pass (Lk. 21:28), the signs and events will happen one after the other speedily. Therefore, like the Boy Scout model says, "Be prepared!"

VERSES 8-9 John had already made the mistake of bowing before an angel and being rebuked in chapter 19:10. Now he does it again. But our God is a God of love and will forgive our mistakes. If I were in John's place, I think I would have bowed also. Can you imagine the glory and splendor of this occasion?

VERSE 10 In Daniel's case, when he wrote about prophecy, he was told to *"seal the book (until) the time of the end"* (Dan. 12:4). John, however, is NOT told to seal the book because *"the time is at hand,"* or has come. People are to be made aware of the future. They must learn the history of the churches and the plan of the ages.

Then they will understand God's program. That's why God had John write the book of the Revelation.

VERSE 11 Here we are told that it will be too late to repent then. Whatever your condition is at that time will determine your destiny. It will be too late!!! I have mentioned it before, but it needs repeating. 2 Cor. 6:2 states, *For he saith, I have heard thee in a time accepted, and in the day of salvation have I succoured thee: behold, now is the accepted time; behold, now is the day of salvation.*

VERSE 12 God's prophetic time clock is ticking and every event will certainly and speedily come to pass. When Jesus comes at this time, he will have rewards *"to give to every man according to his work shall be."* Remember this, we are not saved by works, but by grace. Eph. 2:9 *"Not of works less any man should boast."*

VERSE 13 Why is this verse inserted here? *"I am Alpha and Omega, the beginning and the end, the first and the last."* I am not sure, but I have an idea that He is saying "I have everything planed and it is working as planned. It would be good for you who read these words to get saved now."

VERSE 14 If I were to paraphrase this verse, I would say, *"Blessed are they that wash their robes (in the blood of the Lamb) that they may have the right to the tree of life, and may enter in through* "the gates of the city."

VERSE 15 But they that have refused to be saved are here reminded that it is all over for them. There is no hope! The destiny of the saved and the lost are clearly defined in this wonderful book. It is settled forever!

VERSE 16 Here we have a beautiful picture of the

God-man, the Lord Jesus Christ. Jesus is *"the bright and morning star."* Peter calls him the *"day star"* in 2 Peter 1:19. As the root, He is David's Lord; the preexistent God (Ps.110:1). As his offspring, He is David's son, the incarnate Christ (Mt. 22:41-46).

VERSE 17 Here is a final invitation to those who read these words to come to Him confessing their sins and receive Him as their Lord and Savior. *"The spirit and the bride say, Come!"* God compassionately declares, *"Believe in Me; come to me. Invite Me into your heart."* At least 5 things are in operation here:

(1) The Holy Spirit.

(2) The Bride of Christ – the Church.

(3) Everyone who hears and believes.

(4) The glorious city of the Bride says, "Don't you want to be with Me in your eternal home?"

(5) Your own spiritual thirst is crying out, "I want to be satisfied."

If you reject this invitation, if you consider the message of this Book unimportant or non-essential, or perhaps even consider this Book of the Revelation a hoax or a myth; BEWARE!

VERSES 18-19 Here is a strong warning. What a serious admonition from the Almighty not to take the Book of Revelation seriously! Adding to or taking away from the Word of God is a terrible sin. Think of the many translations out there that have done just that or belittled certain verses by putting them in small print at the bottom of the page.

VERSES 20-21 God's last promise in the Bible is *"Surely, I come quickly!"* That is "suddenly." The response of His people is *"AMEN!"* The final message of the whole Book is *"I COME QUICKLY!" "Even so, come, Lord Jesus."*

And now the very last verse in our Bible: *"THE GRACE OF OUR LORD JESUS CHRIST BE WITH YOU ALL. AMEN!"*

<u>WHAT AN ENDING TO THE ENTIRE WORD OF GOD AND THE REVELATION OF JESUS CHRIST. REMEMBER THIS! WE WHO ARE SAVED WILL BE THERE…FOREVER!
AMEN!</u>

If by chance, you have read any part of this book, but you are not saved; that is you have never asked Jesus to save you, I want to invite you right now to bow your head, close your eyes, block out every thought except your desire to get saved and become a Christian. Here is a sample prayer.

Dear Lord, I realize I am a sinner. I am so sorry and I am asking you to forgive me. I believe your son, Jesus, died on the cross to pay the penalty for my sins and I now receive Jesus as my Savior. Thank you for saving me. Help me to put you first in my life. I pray this in Jesus' name. Amen.

PLEASE WRITE YOUR NAME AND THE DATE YOU MADE THIS DECISION ON THE LINE BELOW.

_____

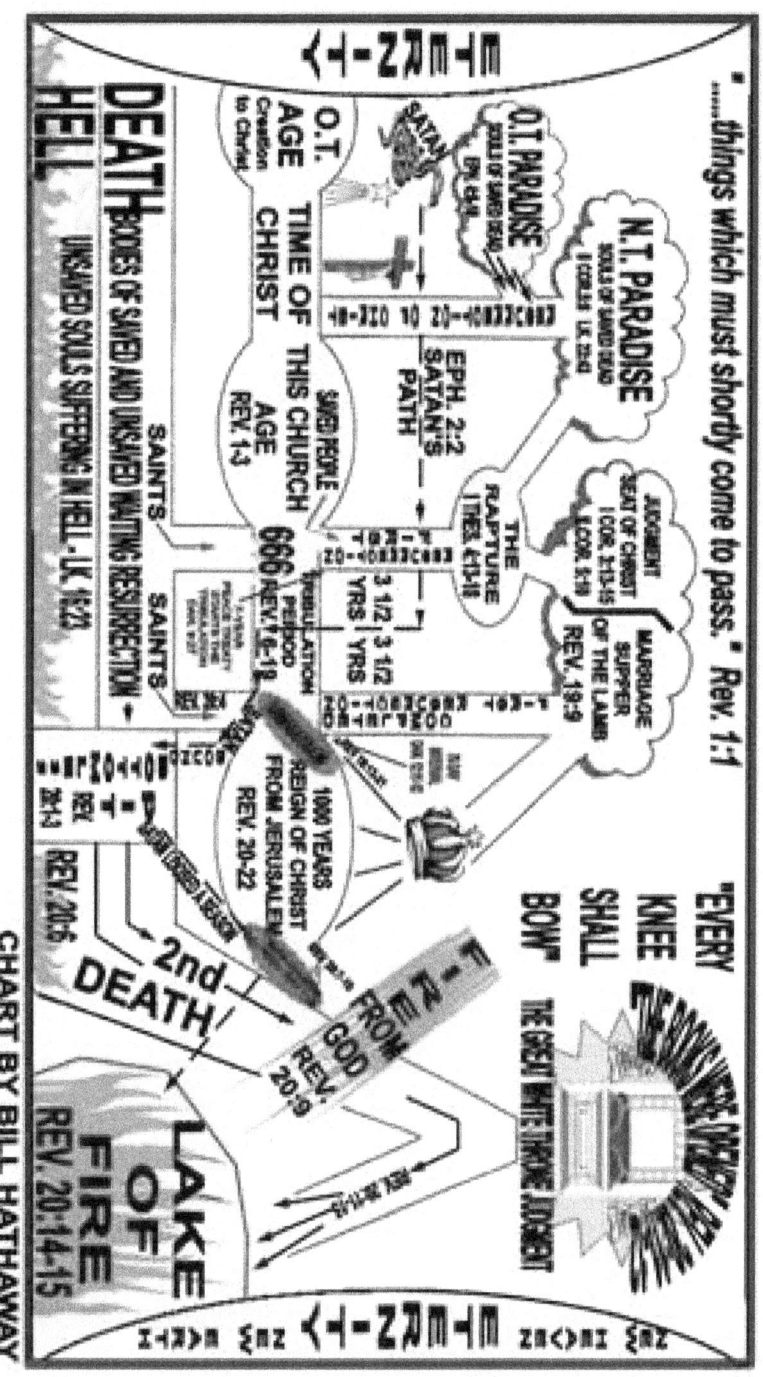

About the Author

I was born in Philadelphia, but lived in Baltimore, Maryland. When I was 5 years old, my dad left us, and deserted the United States Navy. That was in 1935 during the Great depression. A reward of $25.00 was offered for his return to the USS Dale. He was never caught.

Mother could not care for us, so my sister and I were put in an orphanage in South Philadelphia. Many times, I was forced to chew on a rag dipped in castor oil. The orphanage workers told me I was so mean and unmanageable, I would wind up in prison for life, but in 1945, the day WWII ended, I was sent across the street to a small church. I heard a Pennsylvania coal miner tell how he got saved. My life changed completely.

In 1949, I was released from the orphanage and I enlisted in the Army Air Corps. The WWII Occupation of Japan was going on. After basic training, I was sent to IBM computer school. My job included making top secret reports using the IBM computers. These reports were flown to the Pentagon in Washington.

Stationed in Tokyo, I decided to do some sight-seeing while on a three-day pass. In downtown Tokyo I met a soldier who was on R and R from Korea. He introduced me to Ike Foster, a missionary. I immediately felt he was a wonderful, kind man. He was the first man to call me "son." I believe God worked it out for me to meet him.

On one of my trips to see him, I got so burdened for the Japanese, I went to the altar and surrendered my life as a missionary to Japan. After being discharged from the military, while in college I married in 1953. Then after college graduation and ordination, my family and I went to Japan as missionaries.

My wife, I and our four children lived in Japan for 25 years as we served the Lord starting churches and winning Japanese to the Lord.

Today at 93, I continue ministering to the Japanese in America. I preach in Japanese every Sunday at the Grandview Baptist Church in Springfield, Missouri. I also enjoy preaching in English whenever I am asked.

I have no plans to retire. I want to keep busy serving the Lord until He calls me to relocate to heaven where I can serve the King of kings and Lord of lords, my Savior Jesus, forever.

www.ingramcontent.com/pod-product-compliance
Lightning Source LLC
Chambersburg PA
CBHW071512040426
42444CB00008B/1604